The Gift of Anger

The Gift of Anger

A CALL TO FAITHFUL ACTION

Carroll Saussy

WESTMINSTER JOHN KNOX PRESS
Louisville, Kentucky

© 1995 Carroll Saussy

Scripture quotations from the New Revised Standard Version of the Bible are copyright © 1989 by the Division of Christian Education of the National Council of the Churches of Christ in the U.S.A. and are used by permission.

Book design by Publishers' WorkGroup
Cover design by Vickie Masden Arrowood

First edition

Published by Westminster John Knox Press
Louisville, Kentucky

This book is printed on acid-free paper that meets the American National Standards Institute Z39.48 standard. ♾

PRINTED IN THE UNITED STATES OF AMERICA

96 97 98 99 00 01 02 03 04 — 10 9 8 7 6 5 4 3 2

Library of Congress Cataloging-in-Publication Data

Saussy, Carroll
    The gift of anger : a call to faithful action / Carroll Saussy. — 1st ed.
            p.   cm.
    Includes bibliographical references.
    ISBN 0-664-25533-7 (alk. paper)
    1. Anger—Religious aspects—Christianity.   I. Title.
BV4627.A5S28   1995
233'.5—dc20   95-11874

Dedicated to Jeanne Burke O'Fallon
wise woman
cherished friend
forever a child at heart
—a gift to the world.

Contents

Preface

For years I toyed with the desire to write about anger. I began my research with the specific intention of helping women both to recognize the pain beneath their anger and to find ways of freeing their true selves through the expression of authentic feeling. I soon learned that I did not want to isolate the anger of women from the anger of men. Both women and men struggle, albeit in different ways and for different reasons, to accept and express their anger. This expression does not mean the transformation of anger; rather, it involves the creative use of anger.

The announcement that I was writing a book about anger consistently met with interested, even passionate responses. "I could tell you a lot about that one!" "Great! I need to read it right now." "I know who I'll buy a copy for." "I want a copy for myself, a copy for my son, and a copy for my granddaughter—right now!"

This book is not just for women who want to understand their anger and use it well, or for men who want to understand angry women. I am writing also for men who need to discover personal anger. Even generally caring, sensitive men can be surprised and frightened by their own anger.

At a retreat for clergywomen on the subject of anger, I defined anger in part as a response to the experience of being ignored, injured, trivialized, or rejected. One woman, visibly upset by my words, blurted out that she must be angry every day of her life—that simply showing up for work entailed the experience of being trivialized and, too often, of being rejected.

In response to lectures on anger in which I appealed to the audience to befriend their anger, a pastor responded that he had already lost one marriage because of his anger and he was on his way to losing a second. Befriending his anger made no sense to him.

A professor of preaching and worship writes about the discovery of his defenses against anger that led to a conversion. He videotaped a worship service in which he preached on "The Redemptive Power of Anger." Viewing the tape, he saw a "study in control," heard a dispassionate voice speaking in measured rhythms. Everything about the setting said control: ushers parading in lockstep, people sitting straight in even rows, mood lights controlled by rheostat, pristine architecture. "While in the sermon I plead for an openness to anger, both my sermon delivery and the way the liturgy functions trumpet an overwhelming counter melody about the importance of keeping all lids locked down."[1]

Suddenly the preacher's suppressed anger is loosened, and a pounding, shouting pastor displaces his anger onto the congregation:

> I'm embarrassed to see myself shaming my people through clenched teeth for not translating their indignation into creative power. Strange how I pound the pulpit when I get to the part about the peace that transcends all hostility. I feel nervous about the tight curl of my lip and the snide sound in my voice when I rail at those who cannot admit to the lie in their souls. Again, the anger that drives the sermon is too feared to name and embrace. One more time my rage simply plays at Christian concern as an excuse to vent its spleen.[2]

The professor then sought out professional help in order to reclaim the childhood experiences that resulted in his repressed rage:

> Then the surprising courage to reclaim from memory the stinging blows, the fearful cries, the awful shame, the swallowed fire. Then the exhausting days and months when the lava finally flows. Then the emerging sense of liberty beyond release, a freedom to name and embrace any anger without shame. Then the job of being open to others' anger because at least I am open to my own.[3]

Creating an openness to anger—for both women and men—is the purpose of this book. Some anger is an authentic gift that influences individuals and communities to live prophetically. Other anger merely damages relationship and community. This book seeks to assist persons to assess their own anger and find concrete, appropriate ways to express it.

Although the classroom situations (to which the Introduction alludes) provided the more immediate reasons for this book, the deep reasons for my interest in the subject go back as far as I can remember. My father was best known for his spontaneous generosity and wild creativity; at the same time, he was feared by many because of his quick anger. A man with a powerful temper, his explosions of anger kept some people at a distance and infrequently inflicted his children with a near-paralyzing fear. I grew up dreading the expression of anger—his or my own. I am certain that I tiptoed around my father when I picked up any inclination that he was ready to explode. Because I knew anger only as a dangerous emotion, I was an adult before I came to appreciate the possibilities for honest relationship and for work for justice that anger offers.

Studying anger has been a profoundly rewarding experience, and now, what a delicious moment! To look back over a two-year journey and finally say, "May it be so, alleluia, and thank you." I am grateful to many friends, colleagues, and students who have kept alive my interest in anger. The person who has lived with me through it all, who talked it all and read it all, and who knows and respects my anger more than anyone in the world is Frank Molony—a wonderful husband and friend.

At the risk of leaving out names of those who have been companions along this journey, I begin my litany. Thanks to Andy Lester, Alexa Smith, Larry Stookey, and Gail Unterberger for early conversations regarding my proposal, and to Timothy Staveteig for being such a collegial editor. I am grateful to all the contributors to Jeanne Stevenson Moessner's edited volume, tentatively titled *Woman-Care* (Fortress Press), especially Paula Buford, Carolyn Bohler, Barbara Clarke, and Kathleen Greider. I am particularly grateful to several friends and colleagues for their careful reading of parts of the manuscript: Bruce Birch, Sharon H. Ringe, Jane Schaberg, and James Shopshire. Jeanne Burke O'Fallon read every page (except the dedication), sending me both support and challenge all along the way. Thanks to the Sisters Against Sexism, a Women-Church group in the greater Washington, D.C., area, who provided a wonderfully free and open place where some of my ideas were tested. Thanks to Margee Iddings and a group of Presbyterian clergywomen who invited me to lead them through a retreat on this topic; I am especially grateful to Alice Anderson, who nudged me into a more serious theological study of anger. I am grateful to Lynda Clements, Freda Gardner, and Mary Hunt for remarkably insightful conversations, and to Kay Ward for thoughtful feedback after my lectures on anger at Moravian Theological Seminary. An opportunity to work with members of the New Castle Presbytery of the Presbyterian Church (U.S.A.) motivated me to explore further the topic of anger and conflict in the church. Their enthusiastic response to the workshops convinced me that church people need this book. Finally, I thank many students at Wesley Theological Seminary for their interest and lively response in and out of the classroom, especially Carletta Allen, Howertine Farrell Duncan, Marcia Rose Fuoss, Laurie Gates, Jean McDonald, Sally Mathews, Karin Walker, Carol Wilson, and the anonymous woman whose dialogue with her anger appears in this book.

Introduction:
A Call to Understanding

Anger is one of the most difficult emotions that human beings face. It is unsettling to feel one's own anger, difficult to find effective ways of expressing it, difficult to be the target of another's anger, difficult even to stay in the presence of angry people.

Many people find it hard to acknowledge, let alone express, intense anger, and if they do verbalize it, they frequently conclude that such expression damages relationship or community. Having learned in childhood to hide their true feelings, supported in that learning by school and church, people carry around long-repressed anger that surfaces in destructive ways when they are no longer able to hide their fury. Not only are they afraid of their own anger but they also are markedly uncomfortable in the presence of persons who are expressing anger at them, as well as at other people. Some people are not even aware of their feelings of anger and rage, so successful have they been at denying their true feelings.

Hence, many defense mechanisms are employed to deny or distort anger: "No, I *am not* angry" (denial). "*You* are the one who is angry" (projection). "I used to get angry at work, but I don't anymore. I've learned to live with it" (repression).[1]

Once I invited a staff member at Wesley Theological Seminary to join a pastoral care and counseling lab session in order to play the role on video of an angry woman seeking help from her pastor. The first student playing the role of pastor gave up after a few unsuccessful attempts to calm the woman. A second tried without much better success. The level of this woman's emotion was more intense than the students had been willing to demonstrate to one another in earlier lab sessions. The discussion following the exercise was rich. A group of fifteen students, women and men, were exceedingly uncomfortable in the presence of a role-playing angry parishioner.

The issue of anger evoked new energy in me two years ago when real-life anger erupted in the classroom. The incident occurred in the midst of a discussion of gender differences and pastoral ministry. Involved were two middle-aged students, both of whom feel their emotions intensely. Each in a quite different manner struggles with the issue of anger. One works hard at expressing, in ways that can be heard, her anger at injustice toward women. She has experienced blatant sexism in the workplace and in the church. The other has had a particularly difficult time with anger in general, expressing it in the heat of passion in a manner that has been destructive of relationship. He is frightened by his anger, works hard to keep it under control, and tends to mask it with humor. Both persons aspire to ordained ministry, each concerned about how best to deal with anger, to know anger as a gift from God rather than deadly sin.

That evening a class of thirty was temporarily immobilized by a few intense exchanges between two students who were angry with each other. There was an abundance of rescuers eager to "redeem" the situation, taking sides with one or the other student or offering a quick solution to the problem at hand. Contrary to my customary performance, I refused to let others jump into the fray. Instead, I chose to facilitate further conversation between the two students as they took time to say more about themselves to each other and to the class. The extended conversation helped but did not resolve the conflict; nor could resolution have come within that time frame.

In all my classes I ask students to spend the last ten minutes writing a brief reflection on the session, particularly on their own participation in the class, as well as anything they want to say to me. That evening I was given an amazing cluster of reactions to the session. Some students celebrated the fact that the expression of intense emotion could be handled constructively in the classroom setting. A few thought the expression of anger had been inappropriate precisely because this was a class, where the expression of anger ought to be out of bounds. Some thanked me for the way I handled the conflict. Another was angry that I did not let the students take over and handle it themselves. One was awed by what happened. Another acknowledged being terrified by the experience. Clearly there was no consensus as to the value or appropriateness of what had taken place.

I knew I had to do more work on the difficult emotion of anger. Specifically, I wanted to address the need for seminaries, churches, and counseling offices to be safe places for persons to explore their anger. Obviously that can happen only if persons in leadership can deal with their own anger. In addition, I felt a strong call to focus my research and writing on the anger of women.

Gender, race, class, religion, and social location have strong determining influences on the way anger is experienced and expressed. Oppressed people in particular need ways to use their rage to effect political and social change rather than deny that anger or turn it against themselves and their communities. They need to organize energy precisely around the issues that trigger their deepest anger, as Saul Alinsky said, "to rub raw the sores of discontent" until community anger brings forth community action for the sake of change.[2]

While this book is for anyone wanting to learn more about anger, women have been my particular interest and concern. Women in most cultures live with a socially constructed, gender-related overlay of difficulty in dealing with anger. They grew up being told that anger did not become them. As psychotherapist Jean Baker Miller points out, women's anger is almost always seen as pathological. Women are deprived of their anger and thereby deprived of their power. Unable to assert themselves, they perceive themselves as weak or unworthy, as having neither right nor cause to be angry.[3]

A feminist friend reported that she gathered seventeen women who thought they were interested in learning something about feminist theology. Although the discussion was lively and all the women were well engaged, only five returned for the second session. When she asked several women why they did not continue, she was told varying versions of "I was afraid I would get angry if I heard any more."

Angry women who, against prevailing rules and values, risk expressing their powerful emotions often express them in explosions of fury that create discomfort both for themselves and for those around them. Not knowing how to express their anger comfortably, they withdraw. They withhold honest expression of their rage and focus on the effect their anger is having on others, often apologizing or taking back what they have just expressed.

More particularly, women in the church struggle with anger that arises from the theology and history of the church, as well as from its present life, which perpetuates gender injustice. When their vocation is to serve as ordained ministers within that church, women's ambivalence and distress about the institution central to their lives become, in too many cases, unbearable. Some sink into depression. Some leave the ordained ministry, taking their unresolved, unused anger with them. Others seek appointments beyond the local church. Some find a home in Women-Church.[4]

The experience of church women, however, is matched by that of women in many other professions. Societal control of women's anger is pervasive. The one exception to the demand that women contain their anger is the obligation that they express anger in the interest of their children.[5]

The purpose of this book is to explore the emotion of anger in all its complexity. I want the reader to give serious consideration to these questions: What do you do with your anger? What would you like to do with your anger? How do you react or respond to the anger of another?

The theological question I seek to answer is: In what ways is anger a gift from God, and in what ways is it a deadly sin? The investigation includes the psychology of anger, a theology of anger, the ethics of anger, and practical ways of dealing with anger.

Flow of the Book

Part 1 explores the dynamics of anger. Chapter 1 investigates the complexity of anger. An exploration of anger must begin with definitions and clarifications about this important component of human life. Diverse statements about the function of anger are introduced. Some of the inaccuracies about anger are exposed. Reasons that anger is a difficult emotion are explored. Illustrations add concreteness to the discussion.

Finally, the question that is thematic to the book is raised: How can people of faith find ways of understanding and using their anger as a gift of God and avoid expressions of anger that are sinful or destructive?

Chapter 2 explores the psychological experience of anger at the beginning of life. Where does anger originate in an individual life? What systemic factors shape the individual's experience? The work of John Bowlby, especially his understanding of the *anger of hope* and the *anger of despair*, lays the groundwork for the discussion.

A colleague challenged my starting with psychology rather than with a theology of anger; was this not clear evidence that a psychologist does not take theology seriously? My reason is clear. I begin with the origin of anger in infancy because life begins there. The experience of anger reaches back to the early months of human life. Before approaching a theology of anger, one must have a profound understanding of the experience of anger. Is not the Bible itself a theological reflection that followed experience? Perhaps a major problem with the church's teaching and theology of anger stems from an inadequate understanding of the origin and development of this human emotion and inadequate reflection on human experience.

Chapter 3 continues the exploration of the psychology of anger throughout the life cycle. The work of Erik Erikson, made more inclusive and adequate by the research of Carol Franz and Kathleen White, lends structure to the discussion.[6] My hope is that readers will reclaim some of their buried anger and broaden their expression of the full range of emotions as they are experienced in adult life.

Part 2 presents a theology of anger that burgeoned from one to three chapters. The study is based largely on biblical revelation about this ambiguous emotion. Chapter 4 explores the wrath of God. Because of the significance of Christology to a Christian woman's appropriation of her anger, questions about the identity and nature of Jesus are discussed in some detail in Chapter 5, which also focuses on the anger of Jesus. Chapter 6 examines the Bible's teaching on human anger.

In the Conclusion, I return to the theological question raised in the first chapter: How can people of faith find ways to understand and use their anger as a gift of God and avoid expressions of anger that are sinful or destructive?

What I discovered as I wrote is that coming to understand and evaluate anger and finding creative ways to express it are embedded in one process. One must determine when anger is an authentic gift, influencing individuals and communities to live prophetically, and when the expression of anger is damaging to relationship and community. Having made that determination, one must find concrete ways of expressing anger. Anger must be understood; God's movement in one's life discerned; action planned, taken, and evaluated. A three-step model for dealing with anger provides the substance of the concluding chapter.

With one exception noted, the names of persons used to illustrate points in this book have been changed to ensure confidentiality.

Part 1

THE DYNAMICS
OF ANGER

1

The Complexity
of Anger

Anger is powerful, a potentially immensely creative passion. We can compare it to love whose opposite, in terms of energy, is not hate but apathy. If the opposite of anger is non-feeling, numbness, death, then anger might be considered a virtue. Thus, we could define anger as a habit of passionate devotion to all humanity's participation in the banquet of life, and staunch opposition to all that is death-dealing.

> Miriam D. Ukeritis
> "Anger on Behalf of Justice"

Anger as a result of personal offense finds no justification in Scripture. Such offenses are to be accepted as part of the Christian's lot of suffering. Although we might express our displeasures at such actions, anger is inappropriate. The proper Christian response involves turning the offense and the offender over to God who alone can properly judge the offense and its underlying motives and provide a proper punishment.

> Charles E. Cerling, Jr.
> "Some Thoughts On a Biblical View of Anger"

Seemingly contradictory notions regarding anger are readily available. Does the praise of anger sound idealistic; its condemnation, baffling? Placing opposing statements about anger side by side is not much different from speaking with people who belong to the same faith community yet carry clearly incompatible assessments of this difficult emotion. Congregations are filled with such pairs.

For some people, anger has been experienced as immensely creative. For others, anger has been experienced as powerful indeed, but as an immensely destructive passion, the opposite of all that is life-giving. While some denounce anger, others hear its denunciation as blasphemy against the human spirit.

The complexity of anger came home to me when I posed a question to a group of women who regularly gather for discussion and worship (a local Women-Church). I was aware that "feeling words" often are seen as having contraries or opposite counterparts: joy/sorrow, love/hatred, love/apathy, fear/courage, hope/despair. The more desirable emotion is clear from each pairing. The actions that attend these emotions are also seen as opposites: we laugh or cry, advance or retreat, look forward to or dread the situation at hand.

Puzzled over what might be considered the antithesis of anger, I asked the circle of women for their ideas. Surely if I had asked for the opposite of joy, most would have readily called out sorrow; of hope, despair. But anger?

The range of feeling words that followed my query was startling. I heard positive words such as equanimity, serenity, peace, security, happiness. I also heard the words despair, death, hopelessness, fear, stuckness (echoing the sentiments of Miriam Ukeritis at the opening to this chapter). The opposite of anger, some said, is nonfeeling, numbness, death.

These responses undoubtedly reflected each woman's current beliefs about anger, as well as her experience of expressing or being afraid to express anger. To brainstorm the antithesis of anger and not come close to agreement underscored the complexity and confusion people share about a profoundly significant emotion.

At the time that I raised the question with women friends, I had forgotten something I learned in eleventh-grade religion class—Thomas Aquinas's listing of the eleven passions, with only anger having no opposite: joy/sorrow, love/hate, fear/courage, desire/aversion, hope/despair, and anger, which stood alone. Feminist theologian Mary Daly's discussion of anger brought me back to Aquinas. Aquinas believed that passions such as daring and fear involve movements toward or away from an evil that is not present yet is perceived to be difficult to avoid. Hence the contraries: to approach or to avoid. Anger, Aquinas held, is an attack on a present evil. Moving away from it is not a possibility.[1]

Daly finds the explanation lacking and raises the very question that had intrigued me: "Is there really no contrary movement? Where does the anger go?" She offers this possibility:

> Dissociation is the "missing contrary" of the passion of anger. Anger can be seen as different from the other passions in this respect, namely, that when it is blocked, its movement or energy splinters into fragments within the psyche. Rage, then, can be seen as a convertible energy form . . . in women [this

energy] is frequently converted into the production of dissociated "other selves."[2]

The implications of the remarkable suggestion that dissociation is the opposite of anger are discussed in chapter 3. The question to be addressed now is: How has the situation come to be that people misunderstand anger; deny their anger; are unaware of their anger, afraid of their anger, unable to express their anger? I find many reasons, some related to emotions in general, some related to this particular emotion, some having to do with belief systems or ways of thinking about anger.[3] How people of good will discern where God is luring them to respond and then decide what to do with their anger is discussed in the concluding chapter.

Thought and Emotion

Emotions in general are suspect. "Don't get emotional" is frequently tossed at women as a way of putting down their powerful reactions, almost always with the implication that clear thinking is trustworthy (and masculine); strong feeling, suspicious (and feminine or perhaps the characteristic of an unmanly man, out of control).[4]

As a person who feels life keenly, I have often received the message that my enthusiasm is not quite trustworthy . . . just a little or perhaps quite dangerously out of the control of reason. "Wait until you come down" was the message I heard with some frequency from a friend who I thought knew me well and warned me against trusting my highs.

I relive today the profound satisfaction I experienced when first reading Abraham Maslow's *Toward a Psychology of Being*,[5] and the sheer delight I enjoyed in being affirmed in all my enthusiasm. Maslow helped me claim the truth that I enjoy frequent peak experiences, and recognize that fact as gift. Further, his work convinced me not only that those moments are revelatory of the fullness of life and that I can trust who I am in a peak experience but that I come closer to my deepest truth in peak experiences. The revelation was simply holy and brimming with thought and emotion. Abraham Maslow taught me to trust and cherish the whole gamut of my emotions, no matter how troublesome they can be at times. I developed a passionate dedication to helping others believe in their emotions as messages from their "true selves."[6]

Behind the elevation of thought and the mistrust of emotion is a legacy of dualistic thinking. Dualistic thinking has endured as part of the philosophical quest for an understanding of the mind and of human

nature from the time of Plato and Aristotle to the present day. When beliefs about emotions are embedded in dualistic thinking, the emphasis
shifts to *separation* rather than *intimate connection* between one value
and another. Dualistic thinking places one concept over against the other:
subject/object, male/female, black/white. In dualistic thinking ambiguity
about experience gives way to either/or, good/bad judgments.

Instead of emphasizing that thought and emotion can be the best of
intimate partners, dualistic thinking implies that they are separate and
competing. The insinuation is that being rational and objective requires
following rules and standards; being emotional and subjective means run-
ning wild. However, the unavoidable truth is that thought and feeling are
so mutually wedded that there is no thought without feeling tones, no
feeling that is mindless.

Dualistic thinking shapes religious teaching about the emotions, and
with it, parental injunctions about their expression. Most people have
been taught that emotions are to be under the control of the mind—if not
the mind, then the will—but in either case one should be able to control
those unruly troublemakers, especially anger, fear, sadness, hatred, and
depression.

Not only are thought and emotion inseparable but emotions do, in
fact, follow what might be called standards. According to psychologist
Nico Frijda, the failure to recognize that emotions follow involuntary reg-
ularities is one reason for the delay in the scientific study of emotions.
She counters the mistaken notion that emotions and feelings are largely
idiosyncratic by spelling out what she believes to be the laws of emotion.
The first law comprises the constitution of emotion and brings the feeling
and thought worlds together where they belong. She describes it thus:
"*The Law of Situational Meaning:* Emotions arise in response to the meaning structures of given situations; different emotions arise in response to
different meaning structures."[7]

Thought and feeling are not to be separated. Because a person holds
certain thoughts or assessments regarding a particular person or value
(and those thoughts are laden with feeling), she or he experiences certain
emotions when that person or value is present, other emotions when the
person is absent, and still different emotions when the value is secure
from when it is endangered. Hurt and, possibly, despair follow the awareness that a cherished relationship has ended; fear follows uncertainty
about one's ability to handle a threatening situation; grief is felt when one
knows that a loss is irreversible. Anger follows displeasure combined with
an urge to retaliate. Frijda uses the analogy of the pianist, saying that

experiences "appraised in terms of their meanings are the emotional piano player's finger strokes; available modes of action readiness are the keys that are tapped; changes in action readiness are the tones brought forth."[8]

Even though thought and emotion, meaning and action, are never entirely separable, they are distinguishable. For example, to think through a situation or a problem, I use knowledge, logic, skills of analysis, imagination, memory. I stay with the thought, brainstorm with myself, dialogue with another, look at alternatives, try to see connections in order to get my ideas in order. On another occasion, I intentionally focus on what I am feeling, allowing myself to stay in touch with the myriad of emotions that may be part of any significant moment. When possible, I share what I am feeling with a trusted friend. If the feelings seem out of proportion to the situation at hand, then I try to relate this moment to past experiences in order to recognize what I might be projecting from my history. These two processes are qualitatively different; each involves an intricate weave of emotion and thought.

Finally, to understand the emotions, one must recognize the difference between having an underlying emotion and experiencing particular feelings.[9] Having an emotion means that one has the capacity to respond or react out of an available range of emotions; experiencing a feeling means that an actual occasion has evoked an emotion that has effected a change, at least in the person experiencing the emotion. All human beings have a wide range of emotions. The difference is between a general capacity and a specific feeling.

A related distinction is made between the emotional state, which might be infrequently experienced, and proneness to a particular emotion. One might feel hopeful about a turn of events without being a customarily hopeful person. A person might experience a wave of anger from time to time but characteristically be happy and at peace. Angry explosions would be experienced by this person and her or his friends as out of character. Another person is so frequently angry as to be labeled prone to anger or having anger as a personality trait.[10] Whether the result of genetics or environment (including experiences beyond the home, such as racism or sexism), a particular emotion might characterize an individual's personality.

The expression "prone to anger," however, contributes to the fear and condemnation of anger. Some people are indeed prone to destructive anger. Others might be prone to *holy anger*, which promotes life. Instead of denigrating a person as prone to anger, one could consider the possibility that this person has developed what Ukeritis calls "a habit of passionate devotion to all humanity's participation in the banquet of life."[11] If so, her or his holy anger is to be supported and celebrated. May more people be prone to such anger.

Unfortunately, anger has been labeled dangerous, unacceptable, even "deadly sin." Anger can be all of these; it can also be their opposites. Anger can be productive, appropriate, life-enhancing, holy. Everything can be used in either a positive or a negative way: food, drink, relationships, sex, love, play, work, anger—any of these can lead to destruction and death or can create and foster life at its best. My conviction is that anger will only be expressed well when a person values emotion as an equal partner to thought.

The emotion of anger struggles for recognition. As a particularly difficult emotion, it sometimes explodes in rage or violence before its message is heard. Why are there these difficulties with the emotion itself?

Anger Itself

Using an unforgettable analogy, Carol Tavris[12] describes the emotions as coming in bunches like grapes. People do not have one feeling at a time. Ask people what they are feeling at a given moment, and if they consider the question seriously, slow down and take inventory, they will come up with a number of feelings, even contrary ones.

At this moment I feel *excited* about the work I am doing, *pleased* that my creative juices are flowing, a bit *anxious* about whether what I am producing is worthwhile. Buried within the grapelike cluster of feelings that most engage me are *apprehension* about a critically sick niece; *happiness* and *a sense of blessing* that I am in a rich, satisfying marriage; *uncertainty* and *confusion* about how to respond to a friend in distress. I also feel mildly *uncomfortable* because of the chill in the room. I am not aware of any anger or fear; however, if I were to focus for a few moments on the terrible injustices people around me suffer, I would indeed tap into anger, fear, and sadness, perhaps into a sense of helplessness as well.

Like all emotions, anger is never alone. Not only does it cluster with other emotions but it also is a secondary emotion, following fear or hurt or frustration, disappointment or sadness. Because anger is particularly difficult to isolate, it can be misidentified and misunderstood.

Anger can be confused with fear. A parent, startled by a physical threat to her child, shouts uncontrollably to the child in order to avoid calamity. The child experiences the parent's anger rather than the parent's terror. Surely anger is part of the parent's cluster of feelings. The anger is directed at the person responsible for the threat, however, not at the child.

Pastoral theologian Andrew Lester believes that anger and fear are always coupled. He defines anger as a response to the threat to selfhood: to the physical self, the social self, and self-esteem. The threat produces anxiety, which in turn produces both fear and anger. While in some cases anger predominates, in other cases fear is more evident than anger. If Lester is right, then people may confuse anger and fear, denying one while affirming the other.[13]

Following Lester's thought, one might conclude that, in general, men are socialized to express at least some of their anger; women are socialized to repress anger (unless a child's well-being is at risk). As a result, men may lean toward the anger end of the dyad, women toward fear.

Anger is sometimes confused with hatred and rejection. Children especially tend to believe, when their behavior has evoked anger in a parent, teacher, friend, or acquaintance, that the angry person has rejected or "hates" them—that even a parent doesn't love them anymore. Anger is not hatred, although hatred and anger can blend in a toxic mix. Hatred seeks to destroy; anger seeks to change.[14]

Finally, there are degrees of anger, moving from its softened, often disguised form—annoyance—to its most intense form—destructive rage. People can be confused about what they are experiencing: Anger? Aggression? Rage? Hostility? Vengeance?[15] Effort is required to identify the emotion, distinguish it from others, and process the emotion. A person must value self-understanding enough to sort through the feelings in order to recognize the many strands of emotion that cluster within the feeling tones that envelop a particular experience.

In addition to being difficult to isolate, anger is often an unpleasant, sometimes an overwhelming and very disruptive experience. Anger can literally be a pain. One of the reasons people do not like to deal with anger in themselves or in others is that looking at anger is, at the least, unsettling. Try enjoying a meal, for example, immediately after a charged emotional exchange.

Because anger is painful to deal with, people may not want to read a book on anger. Simply reading about it can evoke powerful feelings and fantasies that people fear they cannot control.[16] Difficult to isolate, difficult to express, anger is also difficult to define.

Toward a Definition of Anger

Thinking I had learned just about all I needed to know to complete this study, I read a lecture on aggression by feminist theologian Kathleen

Greider that pushed me behind the scenes.[17] I was then able to place anger in a larger scheme. Greider sees anger as but one of several manifestations of aggression. Her reinterpretation of aggression highlights the bipolarity of this fundamental drive or quality of life, which she calls "lively physical and/or psychospiritual energy."[18] Without aggression, no passion, no endurance—indeed, no anger—would be possible.

While *love* tells us whom we care about or desire, Greider points out, *aggression* moves us toward that which we seek. The challenge is to find creative, constructive ways to use aggression. Aggression results in emotional expression and behavior ranging between violence and assertiveness; rage and anger are options along the continuum. Greider's work provides an extremely useful understanding of the power and complexity of aggression, anger being one of its manifestations.

Anger is indeed an expression of aggression. Anger has been called a sixth sense that sniffs out what is wrong in our personal lives or in our neighborhood.[19] It helps us understand what we really want and care about; it tells us that what we love is threatened, beginning with our own surviving and thriving.[20] People react angrily only when someone or something loved or valued is endangered, beginning with themselves. When disappointment and loss or abuse leave a person depressed and without affect, anger can be a lifeline. It has been called "the last emotion to resist numbness and despair."[21]

As a manifestation of healthy aggression, *healthy anger* can be defined as a response to the experience of being ignored, injured, trivialized, or rejected or as an empathic response to the witnessing of someone else being ignored, injured, trivialized, or rejected. Even though some might label the former selfish anger and the latter unselfish, in truth, both expressions of anger can be life-enhancing and justice-making. Anger is also a reaction to social evil, such as prejudice and oppression and the violence that accompanies them. Anger then is a signal that something has to change.

Anger clearly has a destructive side. *Negative anger* is a vengeful, hostile, sometimes explosive reaction to an interpersonal or social situation that aims to injure persons or institutions and tears at the fabric of society. (The conclusion of this book explores ways of discerning where on the continuum between holy anger and destructive anger a given experience falls.)

Whether expressed in a positive or in a negative way, anger is first a physiological response—it is physical experience. Anger is a natural emotional reflex that is mediated by the autonomic nervous system. One feels angry. There are noticeable changes in the body when a person is angry.

The autonomic nervous system has two subsystems: the parasympathetic nervous system, which calms the body and facilitates bodily functions such as digestion and elimination; and the sympathetic nervous system, which prepares a person to deal with feelings such as anger and fear. A person operates out of only one of these subsystems at a time. That is, someone cannot feel both deeply relaxed and seriously distressed, intensely angry and centrally calm at the same time. This may sound contradictory to the wonderful image of the cluster of grapes, with many seemingly incompatible feelings found in the same cluster. In the heat of charged experience, however, fear, stress, and anger demand so much energy that calmer or more satisfying feelings *seem* to disappear. One is momentarily consumed by a flood of feeling that appears to take over the whole person. Only an intentional pause in the midst of gripping stimuli allows the calmer feelings to reemerge, in which case the parasympathetic nervous system takes over.

If, in attempts to hide fear or anger, a person repeatedly acts as if she or he is happy and relaxed, that person can eventually lose touch with any conscious awareness of disturbing feelings. One's whole emotional life will be truncated in the process.

An angry or frightened person is aroused by the sympathetic nervous system to prepare for action. Although specific physiological changes vary from individual to individual, an angry person will experience bodily fluctuations as a result of the release of the adrenal hormones epinephrine and norepinephrine into the bloodstream. Often the fluctuations include an increased heart and pulse rate, tightening of the muscles and blood vessels in the stomach, a slowing down of the digestive process, and a rise in skin temperature. Epinephrine and norepinephrine provide "the *feeling* of a feeling: that tingle, arousal, excitement, energy" affecting all organs of the body reached by the sympathetic nervous system. The adrenal hormones are the reason that, when one is excited, frightened, angry, or wildly in love, one doesn't want to eat.[22]

In addition to the physiological stimulation that provides the wake-up call, anger includes a cognitive component. The intellect is also in motion, offering an interpretation that energizes a response of anger. For example, a woman has one hour for lunch and makes a date to meet a friend in a nearby restaurant. Her annoyance increases as the agreed-upon hour passes and the minutes continue to tick by. Especially if this person has kept her waiting before, she can *feel* the anger rise—

a discomfort grows as her lunch hour slips away. She may lose her appetite. Perhaps she mumbles obscenities at her absent friend. If someone were to inform her that the friend had been taken to the hospital for a suspected heart attack, however, a whole new set of feelings would flood her body. She momentarily interpreted the lateness as carelessness or lack of consideration. New information suddenly disqualifies the first interpretation. She may still be angry, but not because a friend is late.

Anger includes both a physiological experience and an interpretation. Like all emotions, anger is involuntarily shaped by that interpretation. On some occasions the behavior of another might well be both felt and judged absolutely evil.[23] Child abuse is absolutely bad. Rape is disgraceful and will always be. To say that the act totally defines the actor, however, reduces people to their behaviors, allowing no room for reconciliation. Yet the human reaction may well be to equate a bad action with a bad person. My hunch is that many people want to deny that they spontaneously judge unwelcome events that inflame them as absolutely bad or disgraceful, let alone that they pass blanket judgment on an actor's nature and disposition. Such thinking or feeling is considered childish, inappropriate, and surely unchristian.

But does this not happen? Are not the spontaneous thoughts and feelings that follow a reaction to personal offense part of what it is to be human? The imagination bubbles over with all kinds of retaliatory images and internal sound bites. No one has to act on her or his totalitarian, exaggerated internal reactions to painful experiences, but to admit that one thinks and feels vengefully because of the event is to be ruthlessly honest with oneself. Overreactions are human, just as envy and greed are human emotions, and point to the need for discernment.

I am reminded of a priest from my young adult years whom I considered an ancient holy man (he was probably the age I am now). One of the few lines that has stayed with me from a series of lectures he gave on religious life is "often enough, if people knew what we were thinking, they would call the police." In the heat of anger, interpretations can be illogical, exaggerated, outrageous, even blasphemous.

Not only does the interpretation one projects onto an experience shape the intensity of one's reaction, but different persons project unique interpretations onto the same experience because of their distinctive ways of dealing with life. A person who is used to being in control may become exceedingly angry when a friend or colleague behaves erratically. A person who is used to being controlled will be aware of the erratic behavior, possibly saddened while still ruled by it, but will probably not be angered by the same erratic behavior in a friend or colleague. Rather, she has come to expect to be dominated by others and has learned to adapt her behavior to others, seldom conscious of her anger at being controlled.

A person's psychological state is obviously another variable in the way she or he reacts to experience. Why else would the driver who cuts in front of another evoke a fit of anger one day, an empathic, welcoming gesture the next? (I have wondered if one might not monitor one's driving experience to learn more about the cluster of emotions that configure any particular day.) When people are struggling through deeply disturbing experiences, their psychological state clearly shapes their emotional reactions. Frijda notes that persons with post-traumatic stress syndrome become angry over almost every obstruction, sad after every loss or failure, insecure or anxious over every uncertainty, teary over every kindness.[24]

Working toward a definition of anger raised questions in my mind about what to label so-called successfully suppressed anger. While most people might recognize their anger, whether or not they express it, others have learned to deny that they are angry at all. Is the unrecognized, unexpressed anger really anger, or is another word needed to describe repressed emotions? If both bodily experience and cognitive response are aborted, what has the person felt in place of anger? Is the unfelt emotion really an emotion? A different name might be needed for anger that is not recognized and processed. I have no answer. Christian ethicist Alastair Campbell notes:

> Some people have learned habitually to disregard the bodily changes caused by the physiological arousal or habitually to interpret them as a different emotion, for example, as embarrassment or generalized anxiety. . . . "Anger denied" happens at a less fully conscious and deliberate level. It is a habitual avoidance of the angry reaction to threat or frustration which our first response to a situation has prepared us for. It is an aborted emotional reaction at the margins of consciousness and barely within our control.[25]

Anyone encouraging the expression of anger as a way toward positive change and a more just community must recognize that the expression of one's own or the receiving of another's anger can be overpowering, damaging, even fatal. Its power often leads to injury, rape, death. Property is destroyed in anger. Relationships are destroyed in anger. People are murdered in anger.

My conviction is that the people whose anger is out of control and who injure themselves or other persons in expressing their anger were not respected enough by the significant people in their early lives. They have been ignored, injured, trivialized, or rejected and have not found constructive ways of working through their anger. They need immediate professional help in understanding the origin and depth of their rage and in controlling their expression of anger.

The emotion of anger tells us that something has to change, in ourselves, in our relationships, in institutions. The anger itself is a powerful resource in effecting the changes that enhance our lives and our communities. But whether anger is expressed or denied, the bottom line is that it is often an uncomfortable, unwelcome experience that is difficult to handle well and in fact often results in abuse and injury.

Not only does anger trigger unpleasant physiological reactions in the angry person; it also evokes discomfort in others in the angry person's environment. However, discomfort need not mean avoidance. A pastor assessing what members of her congregation thought and felt about anger asked a group of people if they were uncomfortable with anger. Indeed, most were. One doesn't have to be comfortable with a feeling to claim it and use it well.

Overcoming the many roadblocks to identifying, owning, and expressing anger takes motivation, energy, and endurance. Above all, it takes self-respect. One might first need to revise one's beliefs about anger, which are likely to be the major roadblocks to using anger well.

Beliefs about Anger

Beginning with the child's earliest expression of anger, adults send messages to the child about the acceptability or unacceptability of this difficult emotion. The messages are conveyed through facial expression, words, voice tone, or gestures and involve attitudes about emotion in general and about anger in particular. These beliefs are promulgated especially by parents, schools, and churches. Gender and race, as well as social class and demography, also shape a person's assessment of anger.

The following exploration considers how home, school, and church can facilitate or block the expression of anger. A look at the impact of gender and race on the freedom to express anger concludes the discussion.

Anger and Parental Influence

Most people can spontaneously answer the question: How was anger expressed in your family of origin? Everyone learned to measure the anger rising in a parent. Everyone learned whether and to what extent her or his anger was allowed expression in the home.

Most children are required to control anger, which results in their denial of some of their anger.[26] Primitive experiences of anger are related to frustration at not having basic needs met precisely when the child wants them to be satisfied. Not only does the child not get all that he or she wants but children also have to learn to cope with separation from the very one(s) who could most satisfy their wishes.

Feelings of anger, inevitably evoked in relation to one's first authority figure(s), are too often termed *unacceptable,* especially when one or both parents are the target of the anger. When parents label the expression of anger disrespectful of them, they are really being disrespectful of the child's experience. Psychoanalyst Alice Miller, whose work has brought the significance of nonabusive parenting to the forefront, urges parents to allow children to express their anger without risking loss of the parent's love, claiming that not to do so is the worst deprivation a parent can inflict on a child.[27] (The dynamics involved in the evolution of anger are explored in chapter 2.)

Anger and Education

Clear and rational *thinking* has always been considered essential for healthy living; *feeling,* however, has often been suspect. "Get a hold of yourself; you're being emotional."

Educational systems tend to focus on the right answer, on the acquisition of knowledge and expertise. Less attention is paid to the myriad of emotions that enrich and shape lives, let alone to the feeling tones that are embedded in all thought and knowledge.

More serious still, education that places thought above feeling too easily leads to a denial of emotion. Children in the classroom are often rewarded for having the right answers and rarely for expressing appropriate, even exquisite feeling. In adult life one is often told, especially if one is a woman, to keep emotion out of it. Short of being in a vegetative state, emotion cannot be kept out of life; nor would the effort to do this lead to anything but a joyless, dispirited life.

We can profoundly respect our minds, our emotions, and our wills without assuming that one of them has to control the others. Rather, they should dance together; or, to return to the image of the piano, the pianist would best use all fingers and both thumbs, as well as the full range of keys and pedals. Children need teachers who respect their own emotions and model the honest expression of emotion in the classroom.

Anger and Religion

If children learn in their homes to fear and deny their anger and are rewarded in school for the right answer but not for the right feeling, their education is reinforced by most organized religion. Religious groups have labeled anger as sin, even capital sin. While at home children risk the loss of parental love and affection by expressing their anger or rage, they find at church that they risk God's judgment when they sin through expressing their anger.

Biblical messages such as "Be slow to anger" and "Put your anger away" have a strong influence on religious beliefs about anger. Less emphasis is given to the imperative to "speak the truth" or not to harbor deceit in one's heart. "The power of anger in the work of love" (to borrow from the title of an essay by Beverly Harrison) is seldom preached from the pulpit.

Anger and Gender

Girls and boys receive different messages about anger, few of them helpful or healthful. Traditionally, girls especially have been warned against being angry. They are taught to win approval and suppress anger and aggression in favor of being good caretakers and in order to keep peace. Part of women's caretaking role is to manage the emotional lives of their families, and they are instructed that they had best begin with themselves. Nice girls don't get angry. For many women the message has been as simple as that. Girls and women can feel hurt, but they are not to yield to the anger that clusters with the hurt.

As a result, many girls do not learn the confrontation skills needed to stop abuse. Coupled with the fact that in most cases they are physically less strong than a male partner, their lack of training in dealing with conflict dissuades them from responding assertively in an argument. This can lead to resignation on the part of girls and women that abusive behavior is unavoidable.[28]

Theorists disagree about gender differences regarding the experience and expression of anger. Some studies indicate that females are both stereotyped to be and report themselves to be more sad, more scared, less angry, and more emotionally expressive than males. Women are expected to minimize their anger at the same time that they express their vulnerability and weakness.[29] Another researcher points out that studies show no gender differences in quality and intensity of anger in preschool and young school-aged children.[30]

Writing in the 1980s, psychologists James Averill and Carol Tavris found little evidence for gender difference in anger. Averill found more similarities than differences between men and women.[31] Tavris claimed there is no difference in how women and men experience, express, and identify anger. She disagreed with Harriet Goldhor Lerner's[32] claim that women have special difficulty expressing anger effectively and directly. Instead, Tavris noted that because men tend to use their fists, guns, and knives, whereas women throw things, slap, or punch, male violence causes more injury than female violence.[33] To this list should be added another obvious reason that men's anger is more damaging: men are generally larger and stronger than women.

A team of women who studied emotion and gender drew different conclusions about anger and women (June Crawford, Susan Kippax, Jenny Onyx, Una Gault, and Pan Benton, who refer to themselves by first initials, SUPJJ). They found extensive differences in both the expression of anger and the results of that expression. Men are freer to express their anger and often express it in violent ways. Women are in a double bind: they are punished for showing anger—labeled neurotic if they behave in an uncontrolled way; they are punished for suppressing their anger— labeled depressed if they turn their anger inward. Because a woman's anger is often unintelligible to a man but a man's anger less often unintelligible to a woman, women also hold back in order to avoid misinterpretation.[34]

SUPJJ call women's anger an expression of frustration and powerlessness, believing that "a person with power does not need to be angry." They take issue with the belief of the women's movement that anger is empowering. These researchers found that

> anger was not empowering, rather it was a passion that overcame us as a result of powerlessness. What emerged was a view that if you are powerful, you have no need to be angry. If you are not powerful, and you become angry, your anger is invalidated and you are diminished in the eyes of others.[35]

Some women report feeling powerless after expressing their anger, even when they did so by making an honest, fair statement of genuine feeling in as caring a way as possible. They judge their efforts to be counterproductive. They need help to continue their efforts rather than conclude that their relationships would be better if they refrained from expressing anger. The major reason the anger is experienced as counterproductive is that assertive, powerful women behaving in new ways threaten the established order. Invalidation and diminishment are punishments intended to keep women in their assigned place.

What is needed, then, is far more than the freedom to express honest feeling. A critical mass of courageous women and a whole reeducation process must proceed at the societal level before women in general find their anger empowering.

Meanwhile, some of the emotional patterns expected and found in women encourage them to adapt to the role assigned them by patriarchal society, namely, that of caretaker. Fear of anger and feelings of unentitlement can discourage women from pursuing what they really want.[36] They also accommodate to a lower status and less power relative to men, leaving themselves open to the abuse of that power.

If girls and women are held back from a constructive use of anger, what happens to boys and men? Boys hear conflicted messages about their anger. They are expected to defend themselves on the playground—to release their anger physically when their honor or their family's honor is at stake. At the same time, they are not to express anger toward their parents, and certainly not physically. As a result, they are often afraid of anger. It leads to painful fights on the one hand; it has to be repressed or sublimated on the other. The result has been that many boys and, later, men are afraid of the destructive potential of their rage. They find it easier to avoid emotional issues or to smooth things over than to be honest and to "speak the truth," even when it is angry truth.

Men are also frightened by women's anger. Experiencing the anger of a woman evokes a man's own vulnerability. He fears rejection by the angry woman. He also fears that his vulnerability can be converted into anger. For both women and men, anger is too little understood and even less frequently engaged as a powerful resource in honest, productive living.

Anger and Race

The hideous monument called slavery and the racism that allowed it, sustained it, and has been kept alive for more than a century in spite of its abolition give me great pause in saying anything as a European-American woman about the relationship between anger and race in this country. How can I possibly understand the depths of the rage that sufferers and survivors of racism experience? I can only report what I learn from African Americans. Colleagues and students have helped educate me, and yet these reports give me only a portion of insight. Poet and author Audre Lorde has also been one of my teachers:

> Every Black woman in America lives her life somewhere along a wide curve of ancient and unexpressed angers.
>
> My Black woman's anger is a molten pond at the core of me, my most fiercely guarded secret. I know how much of my life as a powerful feeling woman is laced through with this net of rage. It is an electric thread woven into every emotional tapestry upon which I set the essentials of my life—a boiling hot spring likely to erupt at any point, leaping out of my conscious-

ness like a fire on the landscape. How to train that anger with accuracy rather than deny it has been one of the major tasks of my life.[37]

Even though many African-American families and communities have established themselves as profound contributors to society, the evil of racism is an ever-present threat to their freedom and well-being and especially to the present and future of their children.

Law professor Lani Guinier offers a middle-class African-American perspective on anger parallel to that of Audre Lorde. President Bill Clinton withdrew his nomination of Guinier as attorney general after widespread concern over law review articles in which she wrote of alternatives to "winner take all" elections that persist in keeping African Americans out of office. Guinier did not have the chance to speak for herself before the congressional committee.

Raised by an African-American father and a European-American Jewish mother, Guinier learned to mask her anger. Her mother taught her not to project her own anger onto a situation "but to listen closely to hear other people's anger and other people's feelings. . . . It taught [her] not to internalize rejection." She learned from her parents to maintain her dignity, which has meant separating emotions from content and maintaining her rationality.

Guinier was asked by the *Washington Post* if she was angry over the treatment she received, not having a chance to speak before the congressional committee and respond to the questions raised about her. Was she angry that Clinton said one thing to her, another to the press? Her reply was that she was sad rather than angry: "Not sad that I didn't get this job, but sad that I was not treated in a way we want to believe we treat even common criminals."

Yet, speaking later to a college audience, she became clearer about her anger. She said of a book by Ellis Cose, *Rage of a Privileged Class*, that it portrays highly successful black professionals who feel scarred by racism, but are unable to say so because they believe this would violate the tenets of polite society. "They fear being punished twice," she said, "first for being black, second for being angry." Asked if she was afraid of showing anger about what happened to her in Washington, she acknowledged that Cose's theory applied to her. Recognizing the importance of dealing with anger, Guinier believes that the question "is whether the rage, frustration, fear and distrust banked inside Americans of both races will express itself in explosions or conversations."[38]

If middle-class African Americans must suppress their anger and rage, how much more is this so for the growing underclass of African

Americans who have little or no financial or social power? The unedu-
cated or undereducated, the homeless or inadequately sheltered, the job-
less or underemployed live so much at the mercy of the powerful that to
speak their angry truth is to risk all. While it may appear that they have
less to lose by releasing their anger, they have their so-called freedom to
lose, and they have their lives to lose. The jails are brimming with African-
American male youth and young adults who have found only violent ways
of expressing their pain, frustration, and rage.

No attempt is made here to be inclusive of all races. In many ways oppression is oppression in every race, in every culture. Koreans have a concept that denotes the anger of the oppressed that may speak to persons of
many races: the word *han*, which is best translated as "suffering" or "sadness." One writer describes it as

> a sense of unresolved resentment against injustice suffered, a sense of help-
> lessness because of the overwhelming odds against, a feeling of total aban-
> donment, a feeling of acute pain and sorrow in one's guts and bowels making
> the whole body writhe and wiggle, and an obstinate urge to take "revenge"
> and to right the wrong all these constitute.[39]

Korean theologian Chung Hyun Kyung calls *han* the "most prevalent
feeling among Korean people, who have been violated throughout their
history by the surrounding powerful countries." Especially the poor and
women are without access to power, often without a voice:

> When there is no place where they can express their true selves, their true
> feelings, the oppressed become "stuck" inside. This unexpressed anger and re-
> sentment stemming from social powerlessness forms a "lump" in their spirit.
> This lump often leads to a lump in the body, by which I mean the oppressed
> often disintegrate bodily as well as psychologically.[40]

The challenge of the oppressed is to get unstuck inside and find their
 voice in order to use anger constructively. Because anger is engendered
at the beginning of life, the next chapter turns to childhood in an attempt
to better understand the evolution of anger in human life.

2

The Origin and
Development of Anger

A father brought his two-year-old daughter to the hospital to visit her
mother and meet her newborn twin sisters. Big sister, delighted to see
her mother and cautiously intrigued by the twins, asked her father as
they were leaving, "We don't have to bring them home with us, do we?"

As the fifth of eight highly competitive children, I thought I knew
something about sibling rivalry. Perhaps I didn't want the sixth or seventh or eighth to come home from the hospital—I already had too many
rivals.

Volunteer work in a day-care center for boarder babies has taught me
more than I hoped to learn about sibling rivalry.[1] The center houses eight
children. At its inception, the expectation was that babies would come to
the center from area hospitals at three months of age and within their
first year either be placed with parent(s), relatives, or adopting parents or
assigned to foster homes. For some, this has been the case. Others lived
at the center for over three years. Most of the children have multiple physical and emotional deficiencies, having been born to mothers who received inadequate prenatal care and who, in most cases, used drugs
during pregnancy.

One afternoon a week, a colleague and I spend time playing with,
feeding, and bathing "our babies." Once a week we get a renewed lesson
in "sibling" rivalry, which sometimes borders on toddler rage. Each child
wants the center seat in our laps and once there, anxiously guards her or
his privilege. We have learned a dance that allows the two of us to give attention to each of our babies, though we do not always manage to prevent
smaller children being whacked on the head by their larger rivals. These

are affection-hungry children, seeking what everyone seeks—connection, affirmation, a sense of significance; affection-hungry children yearning for the exclusive attention of a caregiver who communicates worth, respect, and joy. When a "sibling" blocks what they most want, their anger flares.

The question I explore in this chapter is: When did we feel our first flash of anger? The answer is an easy one: soon and very soon.

Anger in Infancy

Our earliest experiences of anger were physiological protests in response to internal and external discomfort or pain.[2] Surely long before we knew our names we knew discomfort and pain, and we knew frustration and anger.

Psychiatrist Donald Nathanson contends that anger is one of the unlearned primitive affects that become the basis of our emotional life.[3] In other words, we did not have to learn anger—the affect followed very early experiences wherein our needs were not met. However, other writers claim that anger is not a primary emotion but a secondary emotion, following fear or frustration or hurt.[4]

The first feelings we experienced were related to a complex of physical and relational needs, for instance, physical responses to pain or hunger or thirst, needs always driven by a desire for connection. In the child's experience, connection requires the attention, care, and touch of another, relational needs that are felt from birth. From birth an infant is a being-in-relationship, and all of the needs of the infant are also relational.[5] If the child's needs are not met, then the child experiences frustration, probably followed by fear and a primitive anger.

Researchers note that three-month-old infants, restrained by a researcher's arm, react with undifferentiated distress. A four-month-old infant reacts to the same frustrating confinement with marked anger and looks at the restraining hand. By seven months, the angry infant looks into the face of the researcher or at the mother if she is present.[6]

By the end of the second year of life, anger is a considerably more complex affect. After a phase of believing in her or his splendid control over a primary caregiver, the child painfully comes to a more realistic understanding of limits. Such an understanding is often accompanied by temper tantrums and sadness.

British psychoanalyst John Bowlby's work on a child's first experiences of separation anxiety and anger illuminates these early processes. Before turning to Bowlby, however, some important caveats are in order.

Reflections on Bowlby

Persons writing out of feminist modes of consciousness continually challenge theoretical material that often went unchallenged prior to the women's movement. Bowlby's basic claim is that the primitive experience of anger is a reaction to separation from the mother. I translate that to read: the primitive experience of anger is a reaction to separation from the primary caregiver or, in cases of shared parenting, separation from both parents or from the parent whose attention the infant most craves.

For too long, mothers have been expected to take primary responsibility in the rearing of children and then have been blamed for anything that goes wrong. In fact, mothers were in a double bind from the outset. If they did not live up to the extraordinary expectations placed on them, then they deemed themselves failures. If they tried to live up to unrealistic expectations, then they met with varying degrees of failure. They could not do what they traditionally were expected to do without becoming what family systems theory calls overfunctioners,[7] a role that inevitably leads to exhaustion and frustration.

Overfunctioners take on responsibilities that belong elsewhere—specifically, they do the underfunctioners' work as well as their own. In the case of parenting, responsibilities that belong to both parents—and in lesser measure, to siblings and to extended family members—are systemically given to the mother. That is, the system designates that the mother will carry the responsibility.

Underlying the enormous tasks assigned to mothers is the belief that they are the natural empathizers, gifted by nature with the juices of care and nurture. This fallacy has been challenged by several feminist writers over the past fifteen years.[8] Every human being is capable of empathy, care, and nurture. Patriarchal values that assign family responsibility to women and work outside the home to men are destructive of men, women, and children.

Another fact that counters the overemphasis Bowlby places on the role of the mother is that in two-parent households, shared parenting is on the rise. The need for two salaries forces most couples into sharing the parental responsibility that white Western history has traditionally assigned to the mother. In two-parent African-American families, the couple has long shared responsibilities for child care, as well as for food preparation and other household tasks. European Americans have been slow learners.[9]

In some cases, a couple recognize the damaging effects of gender assignments and choose to participate as equally as possible in the parenting of their children, as well as in the care of the home. Both to recognize that mothers are not solely responsible for the raising of children and to honor those fathers who are fully involved in infant and child care, I use "parent" instead of "mother" in presenting Bowlby's thought. Using "parent" instead of "mother" also includes lesbian and gay families, where there are two mothers or two fathers, all parents.

An additional caveat is that Bowlby deals with the emotional experience of the individual in her or his relationship with primary caregivers. Less attention is paid to the systemic factors that shape the life of the parents, in terms of both the extended family systems that influence every nuclear family and the larger socioeconomic systems that influence the quality of family life. For instance, Bowlby describes emotional attachment within a parent-child relationship that is lived out in an environment of connectedness and support, something that many parents around the world would consider a luxury.

In most developed countries in the Western world, public policy supports parents in raising children, providing paternity and maternity leave as well as quality, affordable child care. This is not true in the United States. In this country, mothers have been burdened with most of the responsibility not only for the material needs of the children but also for the emotional life of the whole family. And yet in two-thirds of two-parent homes, both parents work outside the home. Over 70 percent of mothers with school-aged children and close to 60 percent of mothers with preschool children are in the workforce.

An added burden falls on women who are single parents. Over one-third of children today will live in a single-parent home before they reach maturity.[10] Many single-parent mothers live in chronic poverty. In 1990, 33.6 million people lived below the official poverty line; 20.6 percent of all children were in that number. This does not include the many other children who were only slightly above the poverty line.[11] Single-parent mothers living on a subsistence income with no network of social support struggle merely to survive; they are hard pressed to meet the emotional needs of their children.

This reality is powerfully illustrated by family counselor Patricia Davis in her article "Women and the Burden of Empathy." Her thesis is twofold: first, that empathy requires a level of emotional functioning that is possibly beyond the reach of most individuals; second, that unrealistic expectations are placed on women to be empathic. Davis uses a case study to make her point.[12]

Anne, a single parent of three children ranging in age from six to sixteen, was abandoned by her alcoholic, physically abusive husband, who left her so that he could remarry. She struggled in a low-paying job to keep her family in food and shelter. Davis describes the thirty-seven-year-old mother at the time of their meeting as "frozen, hopeless, drained, depressed." Toward the end of the first somber therapy session with Anne and the three children, the six-year-old son sobbed, then whispered that he did not think anyone loved him. Addressing the therapist, his mother responded, "Don't expect me to tell him I love him. I can't love anybody. I'm just surviving."

Davis acknowledged that this was one of the most difficult moments in her experience as a family counselor. What she found personally disturbing was her own expectation that an overburdened, defeated woman could be emotionally available to her desperate son:

> Her response to her son, as hurtful as it was, was her only honest response given her life situation. In that session Anne had expressed what she and her children both knew to be true; the struggle to live and the pain of life had robbed her and them of hope and any sense of relationship or connectedness. My expectation and her children's hope that she could care for them in an emotionally healthy way was one more signal to her of her failure as a woman and mother. . . . Part of the horror we may feel about Anne's response to her son is that it flies in the face of cultural expectation that empathy ("mother-love") is natural, is in fact almost instinctual for women; Anne was somehow perverse or unnatural in her inability and refusal to meet her son's emotional needs.[13]

Anne could not give what she simply did not have: connectedness. Without a mutually supportive environment—that is, without significant relationships to persons and to institutions—a single parent loses hope and, with it, the ability to sustain relationships within the family. How many families in our country live in such an environment?

In light of such considerations, it is apparent that Bowlby's theory does not adequately address the impact of culture and society on the child's earliest years. Nevertheless, his theory has been profoundly helpful in my understanding of the origin of anger in the first stage of life.

Anger and Separation Anxiety

Anxiety and anger are reactions to separation. When first separated from her or his parent, the infant is anxious. Where is the all-important provider and protector? Anger follows an anxious, unwelcome period of separation within the parental relationship. When the parent returns, the child expresses what Bowlby calls the *anger of hope*.[14] The child hopes that her or his anger will make the parent feel repentant for the separation and that the parent will not leave again.

The child's prior feelings here include sadness, fear, a sense of loss, perhaps panic. It is the child's fear of the loss of an all-important person that gives rise to anger. If the child has truly been abandoned by the parent, then the child experiences the *anger of despair*.[15]

To summarize Bowlby's extensive research: A young child who has developed attachment to a parent, if separated unwillingly, shows distress. When the child is in the care of a succession of substitute providers, she or he experiences intense stress. Typically, the child first goes through a process of protesting and trying to recover the parent. When efforts fail, the child continues to feel distress but remains preoccupied and vigilant. If the separation persists, then the child defends herself or himself by losing interest and becoming emotionally detached. Such detachment is a primitive form of denial.

If the separation does not last too long, then the child reattaches; however, the memory of the distress leads to separation anxiety about losing the parent again. Bowlby adds that the distress can be reduced appreciably by the presence of a familiar child, familiar possessions, or a skilled and familiar adult.[16]

Note the centrality of relationship here. The child seeks other connections, other companions or caregivers. The familiar possessions, known in object relations theory as *transitional objects,* are initially stand-ins for the missing parent, symbolic presences that ease the pain of loss. The transitional object helps the child through the transition from having the parent present to coping with the parent's absence. The object is a comforting symbol of the missing important person. Persons can also represent the missing parent, providing companionship to the threatened child. Once a child is able to tolerate the absence of the primary caregiver or both parents, she or he can enjoy other companions in their own right. They become "good objects." They satisfy the relational needs of the child.

When the parent returns, a child directs anger toward the parent, hopeful that the anger will discourage the person from going away again. If the parent does not return or if the child feels that expressing anger has no impact on the parent upon return, then the child experiences the anger of despair. Bowlby suggests that persons who become murderous toward a parent are possibly reacting to repeated threats of desertion.[17]

In cases where a child is seriously deprived of basic material and emotional needs or, worse still, where the child is physically or sexually abused, the experience of repressed rage could have long-term, even life-long consequences. While the child represses the rage, she also internalizes or introjects the abusive parent. She then turns her anger at the real parent against the parent within herself, which in effect means that the rage is trapped within her own self.

A child who buried the rage she felt toward an abuser and turned it against herself will desperately need a healing relationship in order to claim her anger. She will need a loving, mutual relationship before she can come to a solid sense of self and positive self-esteem.

Multiple members of extended families can share the fear and repression of anger; such thinking and feeling become characteristic of the larger family system. Family systems theorists have emphasized the tendency for destructive patterns of behavior to be repeated across generations. The patterns continue unless or until motivated members of the emotional system see a new possibility and initiate change in the patterns of family relationships. This happens if the change agent recognizes that things could be different. Often such recognition comes through a positive relationship with someone who offers hope. Sometimes the change begins when a person hurts enough to insist on change and is willing to put effort into effecting the change.

Anger and the True Self

Separation anxiety, anger of hope, and anger of despair all relate to the child's focus on the parent. In addition to learning to cope with separation from the other, the child needs to learn acceptance of the self. The child needs to know and respect the person she or he really is.

Perhaps psychotherapist Judith Duerk's imaginative posing of the question "How might it have been different for you?" evokes painful memories for most of her readers of emotions rebuffed as well as emotions denied:

> How might it have been different for you, if, early in your life, the first time you as a tiny child felt your anger coming together inside yourself, someone, a parent or grandparent, or older sister or brother had said, "Bravo! Yes, that's it! You're feeling it!!"
> If, the first time you had experienced that sharp awareness of ego, of "me, I'm me, not you" . . . you had been received and hugged and affirmed, instead of shamed and isolated.

> If someone had been able to see that you were taking the first tiny baby step toward feeling your own feelings, of knowing that you saw life differently from those around you. If you had been helped to experience your own uniqueness, to feel the excitement of sensing, for the very first time, your own awareness of life. What if someone had helped you to own all of this . . . to own your own life?
>
> How might it have been different for you?[18]

Yes, had each child been heard with respect and affirmation, each life surely would have been different.

Anger plays a significant role in the child's development of self-in-relation. Becoming one's self-in-relation is an interpersonal process that requires the courage to find and express the true self. Since the self is a construct and not a thing one can display to another, true self is difficult to define. The true self consists of a mysterious, emerging sense of wants and needs and possibilities that must be nurtured into being. The full range of emotions will inevitably play a part in the emergence of true self-in-relation.

Anger is an inevitable part of learning to tolerate separation-in-relation, or separation with trust that the relationship endures. That development goes as follows: Normal separation anxiety strengthens the child's desire to conform to parental "shoulds" in order to avoid punishment or rejection or abandonment. The child will give something up in order to avoid further separation-in-relation anxiety. The child who fears that anger will drive the parent further away or result in some form of deprivation or punishment will probably conform to parental expectations rather than express herself or himself in ways that might prove dangerous. To avoid risk, give up the anger, the child reasons. Ironically, the anger is given up at greater risk; the anger is given up at the risk of the true self-in-relation.

Avoiding and denying the anger create illusions in the child's imagination: "I am not *really* angry . . . have no reason to be angry. My parent loves me so much and everything will work out just fine." As feminist authors Luise Eichenbaum and Susie Orback point out, "Not exposing the anger and disappointment stokes the fantasy of the other person being able to make everything better. The anger keeps the connection intact. It fuels the hope that the person one is angry with will actually come through."[19]

In other words, the child fantasizes that the parent will meet all of her or his needs, without threat of separation or rejection. This, of course, will never happen. The fantasy allows the child to deny the fact that the parent is both rewarding and frustrating, that the good and the bad in both parent and child are facts of life. The fantasy also conceals the truth that, though connected to each other, children and parents live separate lives.

The unavoidable truth is that each individual must be separate but cannot successfully be separate without being well connected. The fear of isolation or rejection is in tension with the fear of engulfment. When either fear looms large, anger flares.

A parent's ability to encourage and receive the expression of anger is critical to the child's ability to accept the separation-in-relation reality of human life and the child's capacity to take risks in a challenging and sometimes "dangerous" world. For the child to attain these abilities, the parent must avoid imposing her or his own unnecessary wants, needs, and expectations, which pressure the child into developing a false sense of self—the self that the parent hopes the child will become. The parent must avoid especially the repression of anger, both in the parent and in the child.

If the parent has been trained to avoid anger and has become alienated from her or his deepest fears, primarily the fear of anger, then the child will most likely learn to repress anger as well. So serious is this transmission of false values that Alice Miller says, "The greatest cruelty that can be inflicted on children is to refuse to let them express their anger and suffering except at the risk of losing their parents' love and affection."[20]

In adolescence, in addition to receiving both conscious and unconscious parental messages about anger, young people can find their feelings invalidated by teachers and peers. Professor of nursing and editor Sandra Thomas describes the process in the life of an adolescent girl:

> Invalidation means that the girl's anger is not recognized or is labeled as inappropriate by a powerful other (parent, teacher, or boyfriend). In situations in which she is provoked by teasing, she is told to be a good sport rather than make a fuss. In situations in which she angrily confronts a boyfriend, he may negate the anger by responding with some version of the "you're so cute when you're angry" line. Consequently, the girl feels misunderstood; her emotion has been denied or trivialized. She may question her own judgment of the original incident or become ashamed of her outburst.[21]

If parents did not experience an atmosphere of respect and tolerance for their early feelings of anger and have not recovered these feelings through respectful adult relationships, then they are themselves deprived. Quite likely, generation after generation of children born into such a family system will mask or mute their anger.

Without being able to name the dynamic, persons deprived of their anger will feel that something is amiss, that others do not really know them, and that if they did know them, they would probably reject them. Such persons could spend their lives looking for "what their own parents could not give them at the correct time—the presence of a person who is completely aware of them and takes them seriously, who admires and follows them."[22] A person offering such an affirming presence would accept all of the child's feelings and authentic experiences of themselves. This requires that the adult encourage the child to become her or his true self-in-relation, following the child's lead in respectful interaction with the child.

The parent would also recognize her or his own anger at children who can indeed be exceedingly difficult to raise. Sometimes the problem is based on physiological or psychological needs of a particular child; sometimes the child is difficult out of sheer willfulness. Parents know that some children are more difficult to raise than others. Recognizing one's anger does not mean that either parent or child has to act out angry feelings through destructive behavior, but the feelings must be accepted as real. Then an appropriate use of the energy released by the anger can be chosen.

Acceptance of all of one's feelings is acceptance of the process that constitutes one's life. Acceptance of one's feelings requires patience; it also requires wisdom. Psychotherapist and founder of client center therapy Carl Rogers describes the significance of both recognition and respect for feelings and the freedom to choose one's response. Perhaps what he has offered is a description of wisdom:

> I have come to prize each emerging facet of my experience, of myself. I would like to treasure the feelings of anger and tenderness and shame and hurt and love and anxiety and giving and fear, all the positive and negative reactions which crop up. I would like to treasure the ideas which emerge, foolish, creative, bizarre, sound, trivial, all a part of me. I like the behavioral impulses, appropriate, crazy, achievement oriented, sexual, murderous. I want to accept each of these feelings, ideas and impulses as an enriching part of me. I do not expect to act on all of them, but when I accept them all I can be more real. My behavior, therefore, will be much more appropriate to the immediate situation.[23]

Anger and the Abuse of Children

The combined insights of John Bowlby and Alice Miller, along with those of the women of the Stone Center in Wellesley, Massachusetts, and other feminists, provide an understanding of the origin of anger as a re-action to separation and loss, as well as to a lack of respect for feelings of the true self. Every child must learn to cope with separation and loss. Not every child suffers a serious lack of respect for her or his feelings. However, statistics on child abuse suggest that an overwhelming number of children are physically and/or sexually abused by parents who use their children to meet their own needs.

Psychohistorian Lloyd DeMause challenges the proposition made by contemporary social scientists, as well as by historians, that there is a universal incest taboo. He considers evidence that the opposite is true:

> that it is incest itself—and not the absence of incest—that has been universal for most people in most places at most times. Furthermore, the earlier in history one searches, the more evidence there is of universal incest, just as there is more evidence of other forms of child abuse.[24]

Such abuse leads to rage and fear and hatred. At the same time, abused children need the parent, even the abusive parent, for sheer survival, lest they be abandoned completely. They tend to defensively split off the over-whelming feelings of rage and fear and hatred and to live as if the abuse did not occur, a process called *dissociation*. Dissociation is a protection against the destruction of the parent or oneself. In severe cases, dissociation results in multiple personality.

The growing awareness of the universal prevalence of incest and sexual abuse suggests that a majority of adult relationships are contaminated by uncovered or still-repressed memories of such abuse. If Lloyd DeMause is anywhere near accurate in estimating that in the United States as many as 60 percent of the women and 45 percent of the men have been sexually abused,[25] then the anger demonstrated in adult intimate relationships must frequently be repressed childhood and adolescent rage projected onto adult partners.

Not only are accurate statistics on child sex offenses extremely difficult to come by but the general public is also reluctant to believe what social scientists and mental health workers report, let alone what victims or survivors of sexual abuse report. A prosecutor in a large jurisdiction suggests that approximately 15 to 20 percent of the jury pool in child sex-offense cases excuse themselves from the jury because of their personal experience of sexual abuse. Most of these potential jurors are women.[26] Until further research is undertaken and until the powerless are heard, an understanding of the expression of anger in adult relationships will be incomplete at best.

Nonetheless, discussion of the experience of anger through childhood and into adult life can help both those who have been abused and those who have not come to an adequate understanding of themselves. Having suggested that anger originates in the first few years in life, when the infant experiences separation anxiety followed by the anger of hope or, in cases of serious abuse, the anger of despair, the next question is: How does the experience of primitive anger influence later life? To answer that question, the next chapter explores a particular stage-development theory, looking at the experience of anger at the various stages of human life.

3

Anger and the
Life Cycle

How might it be different all along the way?
Even to this day?
How might it be different if persons of all ages
Recognize anger's challenge
To keep on growing up
Into the full range of emotion,
Into the fullness of justice anger, of justice love?
How might it be different all along the way?
                              Inspired by Judith Duerk
                                   Circle of Stones

Kindergarten children bury their seeds in soil, then water and watch
and wait. This is their introduction to stage theory in plant development.
Next they observe caterpillars changing into butterflies and become
acquainted with the stage development of insects.

Sigmund Freud's psychosexual stages attempted to explain the unfolding of kindergarten children. By age five they had moved beyond the
oral and anal stage of development and were struggling with various
phases of the Oedipal stage, plotting the replacement of one parent for the
devotion of the other.

Stage theory took a leap forward with Erik Erikson's publication of
Childhood and Society in 1950. Erikson included in his "eight ages" (more
commonly called stages) the social development of the person from infancy through advanced age. Today, stage theory is widely challenged by
theorists who know that the vast differences among women and men
within a culture, let alone across cultures and races, make generalization
about human development difficult and misleading. At the same time,
when stage theory is seen as a loose structure rather than as prescribed

chronological steps, it can increase understanding of the ordinary challenges of human life, make human development somewhat predictable, and help individuals appreciate their own processes and better understand their dilemmas.

While Freud's psychosexual stages concerned the development of a person up to physical-sexual maturity, Erikson was concerned with life-long development. His interest was threefold: the physical, interpersonal, and social unfolding of the individual. Erikson's perspective was largely white and largely male; however, he considered the cultural influences on personal and interpersonal development, demonstrated in his work with Native Americans.

Erikson believed in what he called an "epigenetic principle," a built-in ground plan that unfolds at predictable life stages. Each stage is related to all other stages and itself exists in some form from the beginning and continues to the end. At the same time, each stage has its critical period for development. After finding a favorable balance between trust and mistrust, for example, the infant faces new challenges. Trust versus mistrust, however, remains a continual challenge throughout the life cycle. The core conflict of each stage shapes a person's orientation or attitude toward self and others.

My interest in exploring stage theory has its own development. Since first reading Erikson, I have found his model to be useful and challenging and have many times seen the struggles he suggests played out in the clinical setting as well as in my own life. Watching scores of nieces and nephews evolve through the stages has been particularly interesting. In more recent years, I have been engaged by writers who explored the dynamics of anger within Eriksonian theory. Clergyperson Hugh Cleary suggests that the experience of anger originates within the tensions related to Erikson's first two stages of human growth, trust versus mistrust (birth to approximately two years) and autonomy versus shame or doubt (two to four years).[1] Pastoral theologian and seminary professor Donald Capps has likewise placed the emergence of anger in the autonomy-versus-shame-or-doubt stage of development.[2]

However, it was Carol Franz and Kathleen White's appropriation of Erikson's schema that most challenged me. I explore it here for two reasons. First, their more inclusive and expanded theory provides rich insight into human development, specifically on the unfolding of the power of relationship at every stage of life. Second, the theory throws new light on the path of anger. As in any useful developmental theory, the stages must be seen as a broad structure rather than as rigid requirements or lockstep expectations.

This chapter also incorporates the conclusions of the extensive research into the anger of preadolescent and early adolescent girls conducted by Lyn Mikel Brown and Carol Gilligan and their team of researchers from Harvard University.[3] The compelling nature of the Brown and Gilligan research convinces me that Franz and White need to make more explicit the challenge the preadolescent faces with regard to the honest expression of feeling, particularly of anger.

An exploration of the development of anger through the eight stages, using Franz and White's appropriation of Erikson's schema, is followed by illustrations of the anger of hope in action, as well as reflections on the expression of anger in the absence of hope. Because of the difficulty women experience in having their anger heard, this chapter also explores the dissociation that can occur when a woman's anger fails to communicate.

An Expansion of
Erik Erikson's Eight Stages

Believing that Erikson's theory has more to do with autonomy than with attachment, Carol Franz and Kathleen White offer an expanded version of the stages.[4] They find that Erikson emphasizes the development of the individuated, socially connected personality at the expense of the attached, interpersonally connected, care-oriented personality. Franz and White therefore modify Erikson's eight stages of autonomy, which they call the individuation or identity path. They also add a second and parallel track, the attachment pathway.[5]

Erikson's original eight chronological stages are as follows:

1.   trust versus mistrust (infancy);
2.   autonomy versus shame or doubt (early childhood);
3.   initiative versus guilt (play age);
4.   industry versus inferiority (school age);
5.   identity versus identity diffusion (adolescence);
6.   intimacy versus isolation (young adulthood);
7.   generativity versus self-absorption (adulthood);
8.   integrity versus despair (old age).

While Erikson's work began with a strong emphasis on identity, a stage central to the process of individuation, he always saw generativity as the more significant accomplishment—a fact that heightens the importance of Franz and White's corrective.[6] Franz and White do not believe that Erikson's stages, as constructed, lead to generativity. Recognizing the importance of intimacy and generativity to the achievement of genuine, generous attachment, they note that Erikson's sixth and seventh stages, intimacy versus isolation and generativity versus self-absorption, require or presuppose a different set of preceding stages or antecedents. A whole pathway would seem to be missing. Hence they add an attachment pathway parallel to Erikson's eight stages (which they rename the individuation pathway) and incorporate Erikson's sixth and seventh stages in the new pathway.

At the same, time Franz and White realize that in the development of adult autonomy along the individuation pathway, a set of challenges distinct from those outlined by Erikson follows the achievement of a sense of identity. They therefore modify the sixth and seventh stages in their individuation pathway to include what they believe to be the challenges in adult life to the process of individuation. For reasons that will become clear in the following discussion, I add the struggle between an honest expression of anger and the tendency to suppress feelings that characterizes early adolescence.[7]

The two-path model, with my modification suggested at the fourth stage, is shown below:

Life Stages	Individuation Pathway	Attachment Pathway
infancy	trust versus mistrust	trust versus mistrust
early childhood	autonomy versus shame or doubt	object and self-constancy versus loneliness
play age	initiative versus guilt	playfulness versus passivity or aggression
school age	industry versus inferiority	[honesty], empathy, and collaboration versus [suppression], excessive caution, or power
adolescence	identity versus identity diffusion	mutuality/interdependence versus alienation
young adulthood	career and lifestyle exploration versus drifting	intimacy versus isolation
adulthood	lifestyle consolidation versus emptiness	generativity versus self-absorption
old age	integrity versus despair	integrity versus despair

In Erikson's theory, the first five of the eight stages move toward greater and greater autonomy. Then, suddenly, the individuated person is expected to be able to develop intimacy and generativity, processes that Franz and White believe require other, earlier stages of development. What congruently follows the accomplishment of a sense of identity at adolescence is a move toward choice of career and choice of lifestyle, major tasks of young adulthood. These challenges are further developed or consolidated in the subsequent adult stage.

The more significant question that Franz and White raise is how one arrives at intimacy and generativity, challenges that they place on the attachment pathway. They supply what they find missing in Erikson: an understanding of how persons progressively become better able to handle intimate relationships.[8] In both pathways the process begins at the trust versus mistrust stage of infancy and ends with the integrity versus despair of later adult life.

My conviction is that anger is the inevitable by-product at each stage wherein one does not find a favorable ratio of the virtue or quality of life that needs to be secured over its opposite, negative experience. Anger can block the development at each stage. If the anger can be used positively, however, it supplies the energy needed to accomplish the challenge of each stage. The appropriate expression of anger fosters both autonomy and connection, encouraging persons to trust their thoughts and feelings and to dare to be their true selves-in-relation.

Anger and the
Two-Path Model of Development

What follows is a stage-by-stage speculation regarding the emergence of anger in human development, according to the two-path model presented by Franz and White. Reflections on the fourth stage entail more than speculation; included in stage 4 are the results of a study of adolescent girls conducted by Carol Gilligan, Lyn Brown, and their team of Harvard researchers.

Rather than consider here the positive or negative value of the anger triggered at the various stages, the work of discernment and ethical choice will be undertaken in the concluding chapter of this book.

Stage 1. *Individuation and Attachment Pathways: Trust versus Mistrust*

Trust is so basic to human relationship—relationship both to oneself and to another—that without it the self-in-relation cannot proceed. Without trust there is no basis for relationship. The infant who is not able to trust that a parent will attend to her or his needs will be unable to perform peaceably such basic physiological functions as eating and sleeping. Likewise, adults, at moments of pervasive mistrust, might find sleeping and eating impossible.

Erikson said that the child completely deprived of trust in a parent feels rage and is entirely mistrustful. The child will have fantasies of totally dominating or destroying the parent or caregiver. Erikson believed that the totalitarian or authoritarian personality develops in the first stage of life when a child has been deprived of trust.

The child who mistrusts the adult world will be an angry child, with no skill for constructively handling setbacks. Mistrust complicates her or his search for autonomy and diminishes the capacity for attachment. A raging infant has few resources for using anger well. Might there be built-in resources that allow some infants to deal constructively with rage?

Stage 2. *Individuation Pathway:*
Autonomy versus Shame or Doubt

Autonomy includes the sense of being an individual, of willing or making free choices. The child who is unable to assert her or his sense of emerging identity and is instead filled with shame and doubt will look back on the disrespectful parenting and socialization processes with sadness and resentment.

One can cluster painful, shame-related experiences: embarrassment, humiliation, disgrace, mortification, shyness, ridicule.[9] All of these are feelings of having been exposed and disrespected. Shame is a deep-rooted feeling of not being good enough, of not being lovable, similar to the Korean concept of *han* described earlier.

Shame can also function positively, by protecting the values and aspirations of the emerging self when a person knows that her or his privacy is in danger of violation. Shame can evoke creative anger and stimulate positive change in adults and perhaps in teenagers. (I am uncertain that infants or toddlers have the resources to use shame constructively.)

Infants and toddlers who are shamed by parent figures may not yet know that life should be different, that each child is worthy of love and respect. Instead, they experience the shaming or denigrating response of adults as something for which they must be responsible. "Children know only themselves as reasons for the happenings in their lives," says Audre Lorde. "So of course as a child I decided there must be something terribly wrong with me that inspired such contempt."[10]

The resentment that follows the awareness that one was emotionally abused through shaming behavior comes later; its roots often reach back to this early stage of development. Resentment is buried anger or rage that works like toxic waste, destroying one's spirit from deep within the psyche.

Stage 3. *Attachment Pathway:*
Object and Self-Constancy versus Loneliness

The concepts of object and self-constancy come from the British psychoanalytic school of thought known as object relations theory. Objects refer to internal memories that a child constructs as a result of interpersonal interaction. The child does not introject individuals as they are in themselves but internalizes aspects of individuals as the child perceives them.

Some memories of the parent are rewarding, some are frustrating, depending upon the quality of the interaction. A child lives with a superabundance of these objects or memories. The child also internalizes images of herself or himself, both positive and negative, as a result of interaction with the same significant persons. The task of approximately the first three years of life is to integrate the objects into a whole, which means to be able to accept the good and the bad in oneself and in the other.

"Object and self-constancy," then, can translate as a secure sense of the nurturing other and a good sense of self, both products of satisfying connections with parenting figures. To arrive at this state, one must be able to accept oneself as good enough but not perfect, parented by good enough but not perfect caregivers. In other words, the child need not and cannot reject self or parent for being both good and bad, rewarding and frustrating, in order to arrive at a secure sense of self.

To persist in a search for the perfect other, who totally accepts the perfect self, is to remain frustrated and alone. The child did not invent the notion that she or he had to be perfect to be loved. The message was caught in the parenting relationship. Acceptance was somehow linked with perfection. Since perfection is impossible, the child who has a felt need to be perfect stands alone, feeling unworthy of rewarding connection. The lonely child becomes the angry adolescent, who may or may not come to understand that deprivation of respectful relationship marked her or his childhood.

Stage 3. *Individuation Pathway:*
Initiative versus Guilt

Erikson extends Freud's psychosexual Oedipal stage of development in positing the conflict of this stage. According to Freud, the child seeks to displace the parent of the same sex in order to be primary in the affective life of the parent of the opposite sex. The child feels guilty for wanting to get rid of the interfering parent.

Initiative at the play stage in a child's life means far more than finding one's secure place in the heart of a parent. Initiative includes undertaking, planning, being active, without undue guilt over goals contemplated and acts initiated. The child takes initiatives in exploring her or his world, experiencing guilt when parents criticize or punish such efforts.

In contrast to shame, guilt follows judgment that one has acted in a way that violates moral values. Among the experiences that cluster with guilt are transgression, debt, injury, offense, responsibility, duty, obligation, culpability, wrong,[11] and failure. As with all of the polarities in Erikson's stages, the developmental need is for a favorable ratio—in this case, more initiative than guilt. If there is failure in too many of a child's initiatives—that is, failure to connect with significant others as well as to perform age-appropriate tasks—then guilt will dampen future initiatives. Seeing oneself as a failure clusters with anger at oneself and at whomever or whatever one perceives as an obstacle to success.

Stage 3. *Attachment Pathway:*
Playfulness versus Passivity or Aggression

This stage is most significant to an understanding of anger. Franz and White suggest that the capacity to play can be seen early on, in the imaginative playfulness of the toddler and in the child's ability to identify with others. These accomplishments are made through overcoming tendencies toward inhibition.

My conviction is that imaginative playfulness is a by-product of a child's being invited into her true self-in-relation, something that happens best when the child has been encouraged to own and express her anger. When a parent conveys respect and acceptance of the child and all of the child's feelings, the child is freed for play. Adults who enjoy the company of children invite children into playfulness. Children who feel cherished for who they are can freely enjoy themselves and freely enjoy others.

Assuming that the basic material needs of their family are met—and I realize that this is an assumption that people living in poverty cannot make—children who are accepted for who they are can celebrate. They can delight in life. A preschooler who enjoys play with companions by sharing resources and learning to deal with the needs and wants of another child is in training to become the empathic adult who knows how to live in community. She or he will soon be the adult who can sort out feelings, recognizing the difference between destructive, hostile anger and generative anger at injustice. Playing well as a child may mean using anger well as an adult.

Children living in poverty may be accepted for who they are, inasmuch as their distressed parents have energy to accept them, yet have little motivation to celebrate or delight in life. How can the preschooler seriously deprived of basic material needs deal with the needs and wants of another child? And yet sometimes children with few resources do find the generosity of spirit to share meager resources with other children.

Playing well, enjoying oneself in relation to peers, encourages the development of humor. People of all ages are most aware of their humor and playfulness in the presence of people who like and enjoy them. They are most likely more humorous and playful in the presence of the same people. In object relations language, two people at play hold mirrors up to each other that reflect the playful "objects," or memories of each other that they have internalized. When a person knows that she or he is enjoyed as humorous, playful, and good-natured, that person has little difficulty living up to the expectation. (Literary critic and author Norman Cousins has demonstrated the significance of humor in maintaining one's health.)[12]

Since a person cannot genuinely smile and laugh and at the same time feel angry or stressed, humor can be a powerful tool in dealing with anger. Professor of English and Creative Arts Gabriele Rico shares what she has learned from Eskimos in this regard:

> A sense of the absurd balances out seriousness. Eskimos know this. In settling grievances, the angered parties must engage in a community ritual. They must recite absurd poems, sing silly songs, and publicly insult one another to the accompaniment of drums. It is a safe form of letting go, of externalizing anger—a release infinitely preferable to shooting at one another. This ritualization of rage through humor probably helps them to see not only the other person's point of view but also how trivial their hurt may be in a larger context.[13]

The playful child can empathize with the other, can stand in the other's shoes, and is secure enough to share her or his personal and material resources with another child. Playfulness requires openness to possibility and the willingness to risk. In play, one lets down one's guard, makes oneself vulnerable, gives up some control. All of these dispositions are indispensable in dealing well with anger.

The child who does not feel secure and connected enough to play will feel detached, alone, and angry. Passivity and destructive aggression, the downside of the challenge of playfulness, are obvious anger responses. Passivity and destructive aggression are generally nonnegotiable ways of expressing anger. The passive person withdraws, keeps anger to herself or himself. The destructively aggressive person overpowers, uses anger to attack another verbally or physically.

While preschool children can be helped by sensitive adults to know their anger and begin to use it well, parents who shame children are unlikely candidates for facilitating a healthy approach to anger. This help should come from an empathic adult in the child's world.

Stage 4. *Individuation Pathway:* *Industry versus Inferiority*

The school-age child develops skills, performs tasks, and works with tools. From artwork to the alphabet, from the playground to the cafeteria, the child's challenge is to produce and cooperate. Erikson recognized this as a socially decisive stage, when the child learns to work with others.

Without a sense of competence or of the ability to function well enough in her or his world, a child (and later the adult) suffers a sense of inferiority and low self-esteem. Inferiority will inevitably result in anger directed at oneself, as well as at those considered superior.

Once again, sensitive adults can help children who suffer from feelings of inferiority to use their anger in the service of their self-esteem needs. A careful assessment of learning difficulties and skillful assistance in helping the child discover what she or he does well can result in the anger being directed toward purposeful goals.

Stage 4 . *Attachment Pathway:* *Honesty, Empathy, and Collaboration versus* *Suppression, Excessive Caution, or Power*

The school-age child's task is to learn to enjoy connectedness with an expanded world of children and adults. In the process the child risks being honest and, as a result, learns empathy and collaboration. Playmates become prized possessions, necessary parts of one's daily world.

The child without a sense of connectedness suppresses honest convictions and feelings and goes in one of two ways: she either is excessively cautious or uses whatever power she can muster to dominate others. Either she is angry at herself for being dishonest or hesitant, or she is angry at others and overpowering in relationship. The child needs help in expressing her anger that she feels because she is disconnected, as well as help in discovering more effective ways to relate to playmates.

The Harvard research of Brown and Gilligan offers new understandings of the preadolescent and early adolescent struggles girls face and speaks directly to the development and the suppression versus the expression of anger. The study was inspired by feminist psychologists' belief that adolescent and adult women lose their voices rather than risk relationship. Brown and Gilligan's account of the research, *Meeting at the Crossroads,* tracks the "loss of voice" exhibited by the girls in the study as they journeyed into adolescence.

At the opening of the study, which continued over several years, the girls' ages ranged from seven to eleven. The students attended Laurel School, a private girls' school in Cleveland, Ohio. Most of them were from privileged backgrounds; only 20 percent of the students were from working-class families, and those students attended on scholarship.

Seven- and eight-year-old girls spoke freely of the conflict they experienced in relationships. They were willing to discuss bad or hurt feelings, including anger, resentment, frustration. "The capacity for these eight-year-olds to be openly angry—to be 'really mad'—to be disruptive and resistant, gives them an air of unedited authority and authenticity, and reveals their simple straightforward relational desire to speak and to be listened to."[14]

Yet even at eight, the girls were already smoothing over conflict. They spoke of cooperation and were willing to suppress strong feelings for the sake of happy endings. They were ready to retract, reconsider, and dismiss feelings and thoughts. Having heard their parents' message that some feelings are negative and unacceptable—that some feelings not only are ineffective but can lead to rejection—the girls compromised rather than taking risks. They could still clearly express, however, the anger and sadness that came when they fought with friends.[15]

While claiming their anger in peer relationships became problematic for the eight-year-olds, they had no trouble speaking of their anger in the face of what they perceived as an abuse of adult power. For example, they were angry that some teachers did not listen to them or insisted that things be pleasant or nice, that there be no genuine disagreement or angry feelings.[16]

With their inner voices more deeply silenced by the encouragement to be nice, at age eleven the girls were far less willing to express their anger. They had entered adolescence. Adolescent girls are conscious of being looked at, talked about, judged—and they become self-conscious and self-protective:[17]

> Over and over in their interviews we hear these girls struggle as their strong feelings come up against a relational impasse that shuts out their experience or shuts down their loud voices, a wall of shoulds in which approval is associated with their silence, love with selflessness, relationship with lack of conflict. There their anger and strong feelings are associated with danger and disruption. Our interviews suggest girls are conscious and aware of this relational impasse, this move toward false or idealized relationships—at least at age ten and eleven."[18]

Voice training by adults amounts to an education in traditional female values: nice girls are calm and controlled, quiet and peaceful, never aggressive or bossy, and surely, girls are not to be troublemakers. They need not be anxious.[19]

The Harvard study sees adolescence as a time of disconnection, "sometimes of dissociation or repression."[20] When girls—and later, women—repress their anger out of fear of expressing it, they become confused about whether they are angry. They are less certain of who they are and what they think or feel. As Mary Daly warned, the opposite of anger is dissociation; repressed anger fragments the psyche.[21] Brown and Gilligan express the dilemma this way:

> Girls at the edge of adolescence face a central relational crisis: to speak what they know through experience of themselves and of relationships creates political problems—disagreement with authorities, disrupting relationships—while not to speak leaves a residue of psychological problems: false relationships and confusion as to what they feel and think. . . . [They] risk losing touch with the specific—with their bodies, with their feelings, with their relationships, with their experience.[22]

Meeting at the Crossroads likens early adolescence in women to early childhood in men, calling each crisis a relational impasse. Preschool boys have to separate from the intense emotional relationship with mother when they discover themselves as different from her and move out into a larger world. Early adolescent girls struggle with their identity and relationship with mother within a clamor of conflicted voices.

Of particular interest with respect to anger is the fact that one of the most difficult questions for the women teachers at Laurel School was what to do with their own anger and sadness. Was it legitimate for them to show their true feelings to their students? Could they be self-revealing without losing control of themselves and of the classroom?[23] Perhaps the change that happened in the teachers as they became more freely themselves was the most important outcome of the research. If the people who teach early adolescent girls are freed to be more self-revealing and honest, then surely the students in their classrooms are among the first to benefit.

While the Harvard study is extremely useful, I was disappointed that the researchers failed to reflect on the possibility that adolescent girls might quite justifiably be willing to soften their angry voices for the sake of relationship and out of genuine concern for community. Because anger is a complex emotion, easily contaminated by one's narcissistic desires, it often needs to be controlled—not repressed but reframed in terms of larger values.

For example, a child might be quite angry with a struggling classmate's obnoxious behavior but recognize that her colleague has taken about as much hurt in a given day or week as she can handle. The student who is thoroughly annoyed by the behavior may indeed choose to alter her voice to suppress the anger. Surely such discernment goes on within families as well. Sensitive to the situation of one family member or another, both parents and children learn that timing is equally important as honesty. I had hoped for a more nuanced discussion from Brown and Gilligan of the ethical issues involved in dealing with anger within relationships.

The attachment pathway at the fourth stage poses the challenge of honesty, empathy, and collaboration versus suppression, excessive caution or power. True empathy requires honest acknowledgment of and respect for anger in oneself and in the other. Whole persons are empathic. There cannot be true collaboration if significant, even essential emotional experience is written out of the equation. Whole persons must collaborate.

Brown and Gilligan underscore the crisis girls face when they must choose between the values imposed on them by home, school, and society and the free expression of thought and feeling. Anger is at the heart of the struggle because anger is most often seen as a negative value in the process of socialization, especially for girls. Anger is more explicitly involved in the struggle at this stage than in the earlier ones; the school-age child needs to own and then find constructive ways to express her or his anger in order to be genuinely empathic and collaborative.

Stage 5. *Individuation Pathway:* *Identity versus Identity Diffusion*

Erikson considered the adolescent crisis to be central on one's journey toward individuation. *Meeting at the Crossroads* demonstrates the significance of the adolescent girl's struggle to be true to herself and her feelings over against the strong messages she hears from parents and society about what a nice girl must be. A nice girl is not an angry girl.

Identity diffusion is perhaps another word for dissociation. A diffuse identity is a fragmented or false identity. Without a sense of identity, the adolescent feels at a loss, seeking relationship but not experiencing encouragement to bring her or his full self into relationship.

At the fifth stage, it is impossible to speak of the individuation pathway without the attachment pathway. One best finds a sense of identity, of self-in-relation, in attachment, in mutual relation.

Stage 5. *Attachment Pathway: Mutuality/Interdependence versus Alienation*

In adult conversations about adolescence, many people acknowledge that they were often highly anxious, if not miserable, during that particularly stressful time of their lives. Often the sharing focuses on the self-consciousness surrounding physiological changes and the sense of being sized up by peers of both sexes in one's adolescent world, as well as by parents, relatives, and friends. No wonder, then, that the search for trusted mutual friends is imperative to the adolescent. With whom can I be honest about all that is going on in my body and in my life?

In classroom discussions with heterosexual graduate students about their adolescence, both women and men have spoken of the loneliness they experienced when they were in competition with friends of the same sex for relationships with persons of the other sex. Gay and lesbian graduate students remember a far more complicated struggle through adolescence. Oppression by heterosexual society makes the sexual awakenings of adolescence terrifying for many gay people. Lesbians speak of the deep sense of alienation from social expectations that haunted them; they did not identify with the expectations parents and society had for them. Gay men talk about the same deep alienation. They also remember the fear of sexual arousal in the locker room and the consequent avoidance of athletics at school.

Erikson believes that to establish a solid sense of identity, the adolescent needs to perceive herself or himself in relatively the same way as she or he is perceived by others. How can the lesbian or gay adolescent who feels unable to come out to parents perceive the self as she or he is perceived by others? How can closeted lesbian or gay adolescents develop true-self relationships when they find little or no encouragement to be their true selves?

An adolescent who cannot establish trusting mutual relations must surely experience a cluster of negative feelings, among them alienation, loneliness, and anger, even rage. The feelings cluster within the chaotic swirl of emotions stirred by adolescence itself. For many, the anger is seen clearly and then worked through painfully only in retrospect.

Stage 6. *Individuation Pathway:*
Career and Lifestyle Exploration versus Drifting

The autonomy challenge of the young adult is the establishment of career and exploration of lifestyle. Erikson's theory was built on the developmental processes of the male. Women were not expected to shape or develop a career outside the home.

Forty years later, with most women working outside their homes, middle-class young adult women are fully engaged in career and lifestyle exploration. Poor women, especially poor single-parent women, do not have the same luxury to explore career or lifestyle. Their struggle is survival.

Perhaps both the woman living in poverty and the woman with educational and economic resources ask the same question: "Where is the place for me and how will I live?" One asks it literally. The other seeks meaningful employment with a lifestyle that fits.

Without answers, the young adult is adrift, anxious, angry, and depressed that she or he has found no place, perhaps even convinced that there is no place. Whether the person lacks specific knowledge and skill or is unable to find employment for psychological or interpersonal reasons, anger will cluster with other negative feelings about oneself and about whomever or whatever is seen as the problem.

Stage 6. *Attachment Pathway:*
Intimacy versus Isolation

What happens to the young adult who cannot establish an intimate relationship? What happens to half of the wives and husbands in our society, whose marriages end in divorce through failed or betrayed intimacy? Young adults who have not found intimacy through solid connection feel isolated and angry that the vital connection evident in young adult lives around them is not a part of their own lives. Older adults who suffer the breakup of an intimate relationship into which they poured time and energy and which they assumed was based on a lifetime commitment experience anger bordering on rage.

Statistics indicate that most murders and most rapes happen within familial relationships. While the anger that results in physical or sexual violence is an abuse of power rather than a failure of intimacy, beneath the abuse of power is the failure of connection.

I am deeply convinced that most violent people did not receive adequate respect from parents. Their lashing out is an attempt to take by force what was not freely given. Most significant, they did not learn to express in constructive ways the anger they felt at the disrespect and abuse they suffered.

Stage 7. *Individuation Pathway:*
Lifestyle Consolidation versus Emptiness

Adulthood has consolidated around career and lifestyle for the autonomous adult. For most people, career shifts, promotions or lateral moves require periods of readjustment. Such changes, however, do not necessarily result in a loss of consolidation in terms of one's sense of autonomy.

Emptiness is experienced by those who have not found a place in the adult world. As in the preceding stage, the failure to find one's niche will be accompanied by anger at oneself or at those whom one considers blocks to the establishment of a career or to the pursuit of a particular lifestyle.

Stage 7. *Attachment Pathway:*
Generativity versus Self-Absorption

The generative person is Erikson's ideal. The generative person has a sense of the world as community, of all persons as sisters and brothers. The truly generative person is the modern saint.

The person who enjoys solid mutual relationships at midlife can look beyond both personal and interpersonal needs and focus on the needs of the community. Without a sense of mutual relations, intimacy, connection—all challenges of earlier stages that come together in mature adulthood—a person becomes self-absorbed.

My hunch is that persons who fail to care for the generations are aware at some level of the shallowness of their lives. While it is never too late to include service to those beyond one's family and friends in the way one spends time and energy, persons who have lived narrow, risk-free lives may well need relationship with generative friends in order to see the possibility for change. If the person remains self-absorbed, she or he will most likely live with a sense of failure, isolation, guilt, and anger.

Stage 8. *Individuation and Attachment Pathways:*
Integrity versus Despair

Finally, the last stage is the challenge of integrity at an advanced age.
It is one thing to say that the individuated and attached person accepts
her or his life cycle with a sense of peace and fulfillment, thereby knowing integrity. It is another to face old age, limitations, and inevitable
death. Visits to nursing homes most often leave me sad, humbled, and
mildly apprehensive about my inevitable and already evident challenge of
age.

Nonetheless, I can hope I am not whistling in the dark in saying that
a person who is able to accept limits, to deal with the fear of both death
and the aging and dying process, can come to a place of acceptance.
Without genuine acceptance of one's life cycle, with all of the limits it im-
poses, a person lives in fear. People who deny their own mortality feel
anxious at best, desperate at worst. Surely anger and depression are a
part of the despair.

Summary

From coming to a sense of trust in infancy to arriving at a sense of integrity in old age, throughout the eight stages in each of the pathways,
anger is evoked by challenges that go unmet. That same anger can supply
the energy needed to continue the struggle until the demand of each stage
is satisfied.

It is hoped that everyone can point to persons who have met the challenges posed at the various stages of life. Several persons of wise age
come to my mind, one of them being my husband's long-widowed Aunt
Loretto. As she prepared for her eighty-seventh birthday, she expressed
amazement that she could be so old. She knew her equipment would not
last forever, but then, what were her choices? She felt very lucky and
happy to be alive.

Aunt Loretto described a recent celebration with her children and
grandchildren, bringing my husband and me up to date on them all. She
spoke, too, of her siblings and her neighbors. I asked what wisdom she
had to share with us on her birthday. After a considerable pause, during
which I feared I had asked too intrusive a question, she responded:

> Keep moving every day. There are mornings when I wake up and my arthritic
> body wants to roll over . . . just stay there for the day. I don't let myself. I get
> up and go to mass. You know, I'd been seeing the same people at church for
> such a long time. I didn't really know them. One morning I joined a few of
> them who invited me to go across the street for coffee. There's a group of us

now who go to the doughnut shop every morning. (I don't always have a doughnut. Sometimes I have a danish.) I look forward to it. And when I walk back home, I see people along the way. It's a nice chance to talk about the weather or what you see around you. You just need to keep moving.

Aunt Loretto is a generative woman who has met her challenges all along the way. What follows are illustrations of people who face violence and abuse with the anger of hope.

The Anger of Hope in Action

Individuation and Attachment
Destroyed by Violence

A news article illustrates the tragic roadblocks that violence threw across the parallel pathways of a young girl who seemed to be developing both autonomy and connection. Elizabeth Dilts, thirty-two, now living in California, was raped at age eleven by Thurman Moore.[24] Her story of anger repressed and reclaimed is worth telling in its painful detail.

In 1973, eleven-year-old Elizabeth was described as a bright and humorous girl. That year Thurman Moore, twenty-seven, pulled up in his car alongside Elizabeth as she rode her bike to a friend's house in a Maryland suburb. He threatened to slit her throat if she did not get into his car; then he took her to the woods, where he raped her. A passerby notified police, who arrested Moore at the scene. Moore had twice been convicted on charges of attempted rape; this time he received a twenty-five-year sentence.

Nineteen years later, with a five-year reduction for good behavior, Moore was freed from prison. A few months after his release, he sexually assaulted a woman in Columbia, Maryland, when she opened her front door at midday. Elizabeth Dilts read of the attack and once again had to confront her turmoil.

Because her family was not able to cope with the consequences of the rape at the time it occurred, Dilts had gone into a downward spiral. She had trusted no one; she made herself invisible. "Wrapped in a cocoon of hurt, confusion and anger, she became a loner, alienated from family and uninterested for years in forming friendships."

After the 1974 trial and conviction, Elizabeth was still unable to work through her pain and confusion. Her home was tense and without much affection. According to her father, it did not occur to him or his wife to talk with Elizabeth about the rape. At school, she ignored questions from classmates about what happened when she was kidnapped. "Elizabeth kept her classmates at a distance with a gloomy attitude and the appearance of a social misfit." She did not bathe and wore dirty clothes, walled behind her defense system.

Dilts barely made the grade to graduate. She skipped school, watched television, took walks—basically tried to forget the rape, but instead she became depressed. "I just shoved all the anger down as far as I could," she said. "I shoved it down, and one day it imploded. That's when I tried to commit suicide."

Elizabeth was eighteen at the time of the first suicide attempt, which was followed by several others. She went through a series of jobs, losing them because she was too often late or absent. She overcame her terror of men by getting drunk. The thought of being touched by a man has continued to make her physically sick.

Five years ago, Dilts got into therapy and discovered her "tremendous rage." Learning of Moore's recent offense has mobilized her anger of hope. She plans to go to court to make a victim's statement about Moore's sentence at his trial. Elizabeth Dilts wants Thurman Moore off the streets forever.

This tragic story illustrates the anger of hope bringing new possibility to a person who spent agonizing years paralyzed by the anger of despair. How different it might have been if Elizabeth had been encouraged to express her honest pain and rage at age eleven, or even her anger of despair at age eighteen, rather than suffering through a lonely sixteen years before she could tap into her rage at age twenty-seven.

The Anger of Hope
Expressed through Litigation

Filing charges against an offender is a way of expressing one's anger of hope. When the state brings the victim's (so labeled by the judicial system) charges into the courtroom, the defendant has to take responsibility for his or her behavior. A prosecutor of child sex offenses reports that he has repeatedly seen persons who have brought charges go through a process of self-assertion that results in increased self-respect and a sense of justice. In those cases survivors use their anger well, experience satisfaction that their charges are taken seriously, and know that they have done something for many persons suffering similar abuse.

The Anger of Hope
Expressed through Organizing

An example of the anger of hope expressed on a social level is the birth and development of Mothers Against Drunk Driving. Rather than grieve in private, women take their grief into the homes and offices of all who receive their literature. They go further: they take their grief to the media and to the courtroom.

In everyday experience, the anger of hope may be expressed in playful ways. A person can recognize the anger and consciously engage another as a way of staying connected and effecting change.

In Absence of Hope

If one is not able to respond with the anger of hope because the offense has left one hopeless, then the anger of despair or vengeance takes over—rage turned against the offender or against oneself when a relationship feels doomed or has ended. The newspaper periodically reports incidents wherein an estranged partner engages in self-destructive or vengeful behavior in reaction to a breakup: threatened or actual suicides and homicides, alcoholic binges, kidnapping of children, killing of pets, destruction of property—sinful anger of despair, out of control.

The truth is that every person has mixed feelings about a partner. In a healthy relationship, the positive feelings are predominant; negative feelings, of lesser significance, are recognized and accepted and are manageable. The commitment itself, through marriage vows or holy union or some mutual agreement to be in relationship, holds the negative feelings in check. Once the commitment or vows have been broken, all manner of negative feelings surface.[25]

Former partners, trapped in their residual destructive feelings, can become overwhelmed and act out their rage in irrational behaviors that appear to themselves as well as to bystanders to be out of character. In other words, the negative feelings that were manageable can suddenly be felt as powerfully destructive feelings that can no longer be suppressed. As Bowlby puts it:

> Anger with a partner becomes dysfunctional . . . whenever aggressive thoughts or acts cross the narrow boundary between being deterrent and being revengeful. It is at this point, too, that feeling ceases to be the "hot displeasure" of anger and may become, instead, the "malice" of hatred.[26]

Anger and Social Location

The major thread weaving through both anger in childhood and anger in adult life is the experience of separation and loss, which can be misinterpreted as the experience of rejection and abandonment. While the review of the anger response embedded in a less than satisfactory resolution of each of the eight stages in both pathways focused primarily on personal, intrapsychic anger, the impact of social forces influences a person's reaction at every stage in life. A major challenge in understanding anger is recognizing both the psychodynamic and the systemic factors that influence the complex processes that shape human life.

For example, consider the needs and wants of parents struggling to raise children. What kinds of personal losses influence their ability to parent? How have their own early experiences of anger or rage shaped their adult life? A question more difficult to address is: How do larger social and political systems impact parents' ability to shelter, nurture, and educate their children?

With a 1990 statistic of 33.6 million people living below the official poverty line, 20.6 percent of all children included in that number, it is clear that the anger of many people must be directed at the unjust political and social structures that make it exceedingly difficult for so many merely to survive. The statistic does not include the many others who are only slightly above the poverty line. Obviously, many parents do not enjoy adequate material resources for raising their children. This is indeed a cause for anger, which undoubtedly influences the parent–child relationship as well as all aspects of life in poverty.

Dissociation and Women's Anger

One of the great rewards of researching a topic occurs when strands of knowledge come together like the ringing of clear, beautifully toned bells. Such chiming reverberated in my ears on several occasions as I explored the fascinating topic of anger. Many bells rang out for me when reading the work of Mary Daly retrieved my memory of Thomas Aquinas; then her own words added a melody to the music as only Mary Daly can. In answer to the question "What is the opposite of anger?" she writes:

> Dissociation is the "missing contrary" of the passion of anger. Anger can be seen as different from the other passions in this respect, namely, that when it is blocked, its movement or energy splinters into fragments within the psyche. Rage, then, can be seen as a convertible energy form. . . . In women [this energy] is frequently converted into the production of dissociated "other selves."[27]

The experience of dissociation can be as simple as psychologically "leaving" when staying feels intolerable. A simple example: A friend reports that for years she regularly "took leave" during sermons at the Roman Catholic mass she attended weekly, because she was bored by and angry over what the priests generally had to say. Some years later, she moved to a different parish where the preaching was relevant and engaging. She had great difficulty not leaving automatically, however, when the priest began to speak. Her habit of dissociating herself from the scene made it hard to stay when she wanted to.

As part of a workshop presentation on anger, I shared with a group of women Mary Daly's understanding of anger and dissociation. My words met with an electric response by some in attendance. Two women were particularly challenged by the ideas and shared their personal experiences with the group. After the event, I wrote to these two women, asking if they would be willing to put their responses in writing for me to use in this book.

The first woman, a young adult in congregational ministry, reported that on several occasions in her youth, she attempted to confront people with whom she was angry: a parent, a minister, a teacher. In no case did she feel heard. She writes:

> My memory of these experiences begins in early adolescence and, to a much less intense degree, the experience still occurs once in a while. This is what it was like:
>
> On a few rare occasions when I found myself uncensored from within, and, naming my anger or whatever it was that was "wrong" in the relationship, I could feel a very uncomfortable power that would make time seem to slow down so that each second felt like five or six, and I would feel as if I were watching what was going on from a few feet away. I realized whatever I would say was done with great risk, for I perceived I was completely unable to control exactly what I would say, much less the other's reaction. I would feel great fear, and my adrenaline was sky high. I would tremble, and afterward take a few minutes to recover. Then I wouldn't even be sure I could remember all of what had happened, or what was said, although I knew I had spoken from my core, with honesty. I never knew what to call this experience—how to name it. And it was such a disagreeable experience that I didn't reflect on it much—until now!
>
> When you asked at the workshop what we thought the opposite of anger was, I immediately got a flash of something shattering and falling to pieces on the ground—something like red leaded panes of glass.

At last she could cease wondering if the episode signaled a serious pathology. She now makes sense of her experience as dissociation, which followed the inability to be heard; I call it "boomer*ang-er*." Anger expressed but not accepted by the other comes back to the sender with increased force.

The second woman is a retired professional with high recognition and responsibilities in the governing bodies of her denomination. She described a recent event at a denominational meeting, where the discussion focused on the now famous (infamous, to some) Re-Imagining Conference held in Minneapolis in November 1993. She had found the conference challenging and life-giving.

> Accusations were made about conferee involvement, about [denominational] money supporting such an event. Congregational governing bodies were advised to withhold their financial support of the denomination. To many of us, the [leadership] seemed to be allowing a para-church organization to dictate to the church, and their recommendations implied a condemning of those who had attended the conference. Speeches had been made on both sides. . . .
>
> As I left my seat and moved toward a floor microphone I was conscious of several things: first, I was angry and hurt because the "opposition" never seemed to hear us; I realized I didn't know what I was going to say; I knew I would have to say something about [persons who] were all in the room as were many people with whom I had had previous and good relationships.
>
> As I began to speak I was acutely aware that my mouth was uttering words but my attention followed my eyes as I recognized first one and then another person I knew and consciously wondered what they were thinking about whatever I was doing. At one level I felt totally out of control, at another, acutely and carefully attentive and focused. I had never had such an experience before. When it was over I was only vaguely aware of what I had said but I knew I had said it with passion. I worried that I probably sounded angry, maybe hysterical, and that I might have embarrassed my friends. After the meeting I went to a woman on the committee from whom I did not want to be alienated. We spoke then and in the morning and when I got home I wrote to her, naming my regret at having had to say what I did. I have not heard from her in the intervening six or seven weeks.

Here is another illustration of the boomerang: anger expressed, but without response or resolution. First, women must find their voice, however threatening and painful the process may be. Once the anger is expressed, women need support and solidarity. Then, I am convinced, the boomerang that leads to some form of dissociation can be replaced by anger that effects change.

Conclusion

The question with which this chapter has been most concerned is: How do early experiences of anger or rage influence adult life? Some answers are obvious.

If a person is taught as a child to fear anger and is rewarded for not feeling angry, for stuffing inside her or his pain and putting on a happy face, then she or he will most likely continue as an adult to repress anger, let alone rage. Untutored in the constructive expression of anger, convinced that anger is destructive (especially for women), she probably will do one of the following: deny it and become fragmented, blame herself, express it inappropriately, project her anger onto convenient targets, or try to express it and experience the boomerang effect.

If this person projects her anger onto another, then, with considerable fear, she unconsciously identifies with this split-off part of herself in the angry other. For example, she may point her finger, saying, "What's the matter with you? You are always so angry." She does not recognize that the anger she perceives in the other is her own. Until the process is understood, anger might be repressed over and over.

The expression of anger that can no longer successfully be denied or buried takes many forms, which range along a continuum from the anger of hope to the anger of despair. More effective expressions of the anger of hope are straightforward efforts to keep offenders from repeating their behavior. The aggrieved one addresses the perceived offender with an honest message about the effect that person's behavior is having on oneself in relationship. The anger of hope, however, can be distorted through manipulation: blaming, passive–aggressive behavior, withdrawing, avoiding, silence—all less successful ways of expressing pain. Anger becomes truly desperate when the offended person destroys herself or the other in a fatal effort to communicate rage. The final chapter in this book includes a model for dealing with anger effectively and thus avoiding the anger of despair.

The next question to be addressed is: How do religious faith and the theology that supports it influence the way a person expresses or fails to express anger?

Part 2

A THEOLOGY
OF ANGER

4

God's Anger:
How One Question
Became Three

> To be a theologian is . . . to speak for God. It is to have a personal rap-
> port with God, to have a sense of responsibility for God and for how God
> is understood and related to by our fellow human beings. It is to mediate
> between God, as one understands God, and those who listen. It is to cre-
> ate an echo of God in the other.
>
> David Blumenthal
> *Facing the Abusing God*

Theologies are dangerous. Think about it—people speak words about God. All theologies make enormous claims about God. Yet no matter the size of the claim, God is larger—God is more. These words of David Blumenthal both fascinate and terrify me. They sound presumptuous yet at the same time urgent, captivating, haunting. Before reading Blumenthal's book, I would have said that the notion of a theology of anger assumes that a human being can somehow assess or intuit God's perspective on anger. A theology of anger suggests that through reading the Bible, searching the tradition, praying, and reflecting, a human being might find words to describe how God thinks or feels or wills or acts with regard to anger.

If one takes Blumenthal's description of the theologian seriously, then one who writes a theology of anger assumes responsibility for how God's anger is understood, playing the role of mediator between God and others. The saving words in Blumenthal's statement are "as one understands God." Human understanding is never more than human understanding.

65

While theologies can be dangerous, they can also offer grace-filled, life-giving, albeit limited perspectives, and they must be put forth tentatively and with modesty. Perhaps the way to begin this investigation is to recognize that theologies are limited attempts to fathom the unfathomable. No one knows God's experience. Yet for as long as there have been believers in a divine being, people have tried to know God's mind and heart, to see God's face, to hear God's voice, to come to an understanding of God. All attempts are efforts to penetrate mystery, to push the limits of human knowing in order to know the ineffable.

With that serious caveat in mind, I see at least three layers that must be probed in developing a theology of anger: the anger of God, the anger of Jesus, and human anger.

First, the anger of God is frequently described in the Hebrew Bible and revealed through parables and sayings ascribed to Jesus in the New Testament. What the biblical writers attributed to God undoubtedly reflects their own experience of the world and their projection of how God experienced that world. God's almighty anger is also embedded in the theology preached by the Christian churches and handed down through parent–child, teacher–student, pastor–parishioner, and other significant relationships. If God is believed to be a knowing and loving being who is personally connected to the world, then what preachers preach and parents and teachers teach about God's will and God's law sooner or later includes a message about God's anger or wrath.[1]

The assumptions go something like this: God knows the wondrous possibilities for the world God has created and is creating and yearns for those possibilities to be realized. When that doesn't happen, God feels the loss. When God experiences human beings choosing and behaving in ways that destroy their own possibilities or that shatter the possibility of other persons living fully human lives, God is angry.

Most children are taught to fear God's wrath, just as most children learn to fear a parent's anger. Because they embody what is powerful in children's lives, parents to a major degree and teachers to a lesser degree become God images for their children. In that role they can also be seen by their children as paradigms of God's anger.

Aware of the psychological complexity of all religious concepts, my theological questions about the anger of God remain: When and why does God experience anger or wrath? What does an angry God do with this emotion? I use biblical materials in searching for an answer.

Second, a Christian must explore the anger of Jesus, looking beyond the so-called cleansing of the Temple as justification for righteous anger or the cursing of the fig tree as an example of seemingly irrational anger. An understanding of the person and mission of Jesus Christ—that is, one's Christology—will in large part determine how one understands what Jesus may have thought and felt about this powerful emotion, as well as how Jesus may have handled his own anger. One has what the Gospel writers have attributed to Jesus, with the agenda of the evangelist woven into each story. Each evangelist presents a focused portrait of Jesus: Mark's Jesus is the crucified Messiah, whose secret is finally revealed only on Calvary; Matthew's Jesus, son of Abraham, son of David, is the fulfillment of God's promises to Israel; Luke's Jesus brings good news to the poor and oppressed; John's Jesus is the Word made flesh, divine Son of God.

In addition to understanding the biblical Jesus, one has to consider the christological teaching of the church through the centuries, culminating in the challenging contributions that feminist and womanist theologians are adding to the understanding of the Christ.

Third, and perhaps more difficult to ascertain than the anger of God and the anger of Jesus, is what God and Jesus think about human anger—both anger at God and anger in general: at parents, oneself, other persons, events, institutions. To understand human anger theologically, I return to the Bible for evidence and insight. What does the Bible say about human anger toward God and toward others? What does one learn from the angry people in the Bible?

The Christian tradition has largely been shaped by ongoing theological reflection on the Bible. In turn, tradition shapes believers' attitudes toward anger at God, as well as toward human anger. The church's teaching about human anger is included in the exploration.

The task of developing a theology of anger is large and at the same time engaging. This chapter explores the anger of God in the Bible, offering six possible interpretations of God's wrath. It is my belief that a christological exploration is needed before one can focus on the anger of Jesus. Hence chapter 5 has two major foci: one's appropriation of Christology, or an individual's answer to the question Jesus asked of Peter, "Who do you say that I am?"; and an exploration of the anger of Jesus as revealed or concealed in the Gospel stories. Human anger at God and at others as well as the Christian tradition's teachings about anger are explored in chapter 6.

God's Anger

A caricature of the Bible that many Christians grew up with portrays the God of the Hebrew Bible as an angry, punitive God, whereas the God of the New Testament is a God of love. Anyone who takes the Bible seriously knows that, from Genesis through Revelation, the books of the Bible present far more complex, more nuanced images of the Holy One than this portrayal.

Words conveying anger are woven throughout the Hebrew Bible. The word used most frequently (224 times) for anger doubles as the word for nose and is used to express snorting or despising someone. Next in frequency are a word meaning "to burn or glow" (136 times) and, closely related, a word meaning "to be hot" (118 occurrences). Other meanings include: to curse or scold; to grieve or be discontent; to be provoked or annoyed; to break out; to tremble or be excited; and finally, there is also a word that refers to moving air.[2] Indeed, anger is an important component of human life and a significant aspect of the biblical presentation of the Holy One.

Proportionate to the respective lengths of the Hebrew Bible and the New Testament, there may be as much allusion to the wrath of God in the New Testament as in the Hebrew Bible.[3] Jesus refers to the anger of God only once, but through parables and sayings, one receives messages about a God who loves justice and hates evil. The epistles, especially Romans and 1 Corinthians, elaborate on the God of wrath.

The overall biblical message is clear: God becomes enraged. The scriptures portray a God who acts out of unchallengeable power, who acts arbitrarily, even vengefully. Most believers are accustomed to gloss over these portrayals.

An abundance of proof texts could be offered to illustrate that the God of the Hebrew people is both a loving God and an angry God. While the texts depicting a God of love may be problematic for those who have not experienced adequate acceptance and love, as well as for those who have experienced betrayal through serious abuse, the texts depicting a wrathful God are stumbling blocks for many people of religious faith. What does one do with these portrayals of God? How does one interpret the Hebrew Bible and New Testament descriptions of divine wrath?

I find six possible interpretations, some having to do with the nature or attributes of God, others with human nature, and a final one relative to both God's nature and human nature. I begin with the most outrageous, an interpretation elaborated by David Blumenthal in his profoundly challenging study *Facing the Abusing God: A Theology of Protest.*

Interpretation 1.
The Biblical God Is an Abuser

Blumenthal proposes, "We must begin, under the seal of truth, by admitting that Scripture does indeed portray God as an abusing person; that God, as agent in our sacred texts, does indeed act abusively; that God, as described in the Bible, acts like an abusing male: husband, father, and lord."[4] God is hostile, even arbitrary in the use of power—one might say God is demonic.[5] Perhaps everyone would admit that the God of the Hebrew Bible, as well as the God proclaimed in the New Testament, is at times a wrathful God. Yet few would call God's rage abusive.

It is a mistake to impose a literal reading on biblical materials that were composed out of a prescientific, mythic consciousness. Even allowing for the vast differences between the way the biblical writers perceived both seen and unseen reality and the way twentieth-century readers do, many of the images of God presented in the Hebrew Bible are troubling. Take Numbers 16:1–35, for example. The passage recounts a revolt in the ranks while Moses wandered in the wilderness with the Israelites. Moses warned that God would open the ground and the rebels would be swallowed alive. And so it happened—250 men and their households perished. Why? Because the men wanted to share the priesthood with Moses.

In 1 Samuel 15, Samuel tells Saul that God will use him as an agent to carry out the punishment of the Amalekites for opposing the Israelites: "Now go and attack Amalek, and utterly destroy all that they have; do not spare them, but kill both man and woman, child and infant, ox and sheep, camel and donkey" (15:3). For strategic purposes, however, Saul spared King Agag and the best of his animals. He kept the things that were of value to him, yet killed the women and children. He also spared the Kenites, who had been good to the Israelites. In other words, he selectively ravaged and, in so doing, did not practice blind obedience. The Lord was dissatisfied and directed Samuel to remove Saul from office. In contrast to Saul, obedient Samuel proved himself a letter-of-the-law man: he "hewed Agag in pieces before the Lord in Gilgal" (1 Sam. 15:33b).

God punishes excessively, as in 2 Samuel 6, where Uzzah is struck dead when he touches the ark in order to protect it after it was shaken by oxen. The central message seems to be that the ark is a sign or expression of the unapproachable otherness of Yahweh, a sacred object to which persons draw near at their own peril. Ethical considerations are not part of the picture of this kind of thinking. Nonetheless, the writers are speaking of the use of power by the All Powerful. Does the innocent touching of any sacred object warrant such punishment?

The prophets speak of a vindictive God who will "pay back his anger in fury" (Isa. 66:15), who will make false prophets "eat wormwood, and give them poisonous water to drink" (Jer. 23:15). God is abusive; Blumenthal says:

> God *is* a sadist/abusing parent in Jewish and Christian tradition—God does stand by while God's son is whipped and crucified, even though God is empowered! . . . And we, too, are sadists/abusers, because God and we are in one image. *But* neither God nor we are like that *always,* which is why God and we have not destroyed one another (yet).[6]

To cite Blumenthal out of context is perhaps unfair to him and to readers. His post-Holocaust theology, which includes the perspective of the adult survivor of child abuse, never lets God off the hook. Blumenthal's book is rich and challenging; I would say it is haunting.

In the end, however, I must part ways with Blumenthal's conclusions. My faith in a God whose central purpose and energy and activity are love rules out the possibility that God is abusive. God's world is full of abuse, but God, whom philosophers describe as truth, goodness, and beauty, is the first to despise abuse. If I agreed with David Blumenthal that God is abusive, then I would be unable to keep alive faith in God. Might it be that Blumenthal has a too-literal interpretation of the Hebrew Bible's presentation of God's activity on behalf of Israel, thus assuming that the God who parted the Red Sea could surely have freed God's people from the concentration camps? The same all-powerful God would also protect innocent children from the hands of abusive adults.

The wrath of God is announced early in the Gospel narratives. In Luke and Matthew, John the Baptist addresses the crowds that came to him: "You brood of vipers! Who warned you to flee from the wrath to come?" (Matt. 3:7; Luke 3:7). In John's Gospel, it is Jesus who warns that "whoever disobeys the Son will not see life, but must endure God's wrath" (John 3:36).

In Romans, one is warned that in judging others, "by your hard and impenitent heart you are storing up wrath for yourself on the day of wrath, when God's righteous judgment will be revealed" (Rom. 2:5; cf 1:18). The many references in the New Testament to the day of judgment can be read as the plan of an abusing God. Descriptions are heavy with destruction: corpses and vultures (Luke 17:37), people crushed and ruined (Luke 19:44), unquenchable fire (Matt. 25:41, 46; Mark 9:43; Luke 3:17), a quick and decisive execution of sentence (Rom. 9:28). It would be better to be maimed or lame now than to receive the judgment on the day of wrath (Matt. 18:8–9; Mark 9:43–48).

Again, I bring a literal consciousness to the passages that were written to illustrate the unfathomable power of God. These are the images, however, that convey to children and adults alike that God is terrible in God's wrath.

Many of the parables the evangelists ascribe to Jesus speak indirectly of the end time, especially parables about the kingdom of heaven. Weeds are burned; evildoers are thrown into furnaces; bad fish are tossed out; the angels separate evil from righteous, throwing evil into the furnace (Matt. 13:30–50). The collective wars of the warring world come to mind when I read, "Then comes the end, when [Christ] hands over the kingdom to God the Father, after he has destroyed every ruler and every authority and power. For he must reign until he has put all his enemies under his feet" (1 Cor. 15:24–25).

What kind of God needs to prove right and might in this manner? Perhaps the texts are far more about human life than about divine activity. Maybe these are expressions of just how serious human history is, hyperbolic warnings that how one lives and orients oneself has ultimate consequences.

In the Gospel accounts, Jesus makes only one direct reference to God's anger, when predicting what the wrathful God will do when Jerusalem falls. Everyone will be in danger:

> When you see Jerusalem surrounded by armies, then know that its desolation has come near. Then those in Judea must flee to the mountains, and those inside the city must leave it, and those out in the country must not enter it; for these are days of vengeance, as a fulfillment of all that is written. Woe to those who are pregnant and to those who are nursing infants in those days! For there will be great distress on the earth and wrath against this people. (Luke 21:20–23)

Aware of my struggle with the punitive God of the Bible, a colleague asked me how the divine reaction to human evil should be expressed. Is it godlike or the antithesis of God to want child sex offenders punished? Remember Ivan in Fyodor Dostoyevsky's *The Brothers Karamazov*, who would not go into a heaven that forgave the landowner who had his dogs tear a child to pieces; Ivan was more scandalized by divine forgiveness than by divine punishment. "Is there a place for punishment in your world," my friend asked, "whether here and now or eschatologically?"

I want people to take responsibility for their actions, which amounts to just punishment. Yet even as I say that, I know that the sins of one generation are visited on the next, making it humanly impossible to trace responsibility for evil to its true source. Disrespected people abuse out of their abusive histories. I want my God to lure everyone—and all are sinners in need of the lure—to justice-love.

Perhaps theories of atonement evolved out of the same basic question my colleague put to me: How are evildoers punished? When the offense is a direct refusal to follow God's command, how does the sinner repent? The tradition believed that God was so powerfully angry that only God could initiate atonement. Somehow, in a divine calculus, divine justice needed an infinite recompense for the infinite dishonor done by human disobedience. Hence the tradition provided theories explaining that after Adam and Eve's fall, humankind could be brought back to God only when one of its own, who was God's own, paid the debt. The abuse done to God was repaired by God's innocent child.

Christian theologies of atonement have themselves been labeled by feminist theologians and others as abusive. Joanne Carlson Brown and Rebecca Parker describe such theories as "divine child abuse . . . paraded as salvific."[7] After reviewing several theories of atonement, Brown and Parker conclude that "Christianity is an abusive theology that glorifies suffering."[8]

The Markan Jesus gives his life as "a ransom for many" (Mark 10:45). Only a boundlessly angry or totally narcissistic God would make such a demand. Is it as the epistle to the Romans claims, that "judgment following one trespass brought condemnation" (Rom. 5:16)? One trespass and the condemnation of all? One trespass and the sacrifice of God's child?

The Johannine Jesus questions whether he is to ask God to save him from his hour of death and answers, "No, it is for this reason that I have come to this hour. Father, glorify your name" (John 12:27–28). Surely Jesus had to die, but was an untimely, torturous agony and death necessary for God to be glorified?

In the first epistle of John, one reads that God is love, and that such love is revealed through God's sending God's only son as "the atoning sacrifice for our sins" (1 John 4:10; cf. Rom. 8:32). Was this an instance of divine child abuse?

Reading these many texts as indications that God is abusive is but one alternative. Considering the distinction between the anger of despair and the anger of hope discussed earlier, one might say that abusive anger is the anger of despair. But there is also the anger of hope, the anger aimed at effecting change and establishing a mutually satisfying relation-

ship. The anger of hope is anger held in tension with love. The second interpretation to be considered is that God's anger is always balanced by
God's love.

Interpretation 2.
God's Anger Is in Tension with God's Love

Put another way, anger and compassion are God's twin attitudes.
Compassion is the primary reason for God and for everyone to be slow to
anger.[9] God is not an abusive God; what may appear abusive is not. When
God punishes God's people, God expresses the anger of hope that must
always be seen as part of God's passion for human well-being. God's
anger and God's love are balancing expressions of God's power.

Dominant emphases in the Hebrew Bible are that humankind is responsible for evil and that evil justifies divine wrath. Because God cannot
tolerate wrongdoing, out of justice God must wreak vengeance—not out
of malice or evil intent.[10] One might consider the same texts noted to illustrate the abusive God and say that what appears to be abusive is an expression of God's justice-love. It is true that Isaiah says God "will come
in fire . . . to pay back his anger in fury" (Isa. 66:15), but he also speaks
for God saying, "As a mother comforts her child, so I will comfort you"
(66:13).

Not only is God's anger in tension with God's compassion, but the
prophet Hosea promises that God's love will finally tip the balance:

> When Israel was a child, I loved him. . . . I took them up in my arms; but they
> did not know that I healed them. . . . How can I give you up, Ephraim? . . . My
> heart recoils within me; my compassion grows warm and tender. I will not ex-
> ecute my fierce anger . . . for I am God and no mortal, the Holy One in your
> midst, and I will not come in wrath." (Hos. 11:1, 3, 8–9).

A God whose love is held in tension with God's anger is also alluded to in
the Gospel accounts of Jesus. Speaking of divine punishment to those
who harm children, Jesus suggests that God's love for children cannot
tolerate abuse of them: "If any of you put a stumbling block before one of
these little ones who believe in me, it would be better for you if a great
millstone were fastened around your neck and you were drowned in the
depth of the sea" (Matt. 18:6).

The emphasis in this interpretation is on the large picture of God in
relation to humankind. God cares for all and is instructing and guiding
both Israel and humankind on how to live justice-love. The analogy
between God and humankind, on the one hand, and an adult and child,

on the other, need not imply that human beings are dependent children seeking a parent's instruction. Rather, the analogy speaks of the enormous responsibility for and power adults have over the children whose lives are in their hands; this alongside the infinite love God has for both the adult and the child. God disciplines only because God loves.

One serious risk in saying that God disciplines only because God loves is that adults can claim that they do the same, using God's wrath as a rationalization for the abusive disciplining of children. In many cases the persons disciplined are not guilty of wrongdoing; they are innocent people subject to the abuse of power. "I must punish you because I love you." "My anger is always in tension with my love." Or as Alice Miller wrote in her book by the same title, this is "for your own good."[11] And God can be claimed as the model for the abuse of power.

Shift the focus a bit, from the God who is both loving and angry to the people who now follow and now disobey. In other words, the anger of God described by the biblical writer has less to do with the nature of God than with the behavior of God's people.

Interpretation 3.
God's Wrath Is God's Way of Punishing
God's People for Their Disobedience

The anger and compassion of God reappear in light of the covenant or contract between God and God's people. If you commit an evil deed, then you pay the consequences: an eye for an eye; a tooth for a tooth. People are instructed; people break the rules. Yahweh judges; Yahweh punishes.

Moses delivered an exacting law to the people of Israel. With it came the warning: "If you will not obey me, and do not observe all these commandments . . . I in turn will do this to you: I will bring terror on you; consumption and fever that waste the eyes and cause life to pine away" (Lev. 26:14, 16). The same type of warning appears in Deuteronomy: "The Lord will send upon you disaster, panic, and frustration in everything you attempt to do, until you are destroyed and perish quickly, on account of the evil of your deeds, because you have forsaken me" (Deut. 28:20).

In Jeremiah 44, the God of Israel declares that barrenness in Jericho and the towns of Judah is a result of God's anger at disobedience:

> But they did not listen or incline their ear, to turn from their wickedness and make no offerings to other gods. So my wrath and my anger were poured out and kindled in the towns of Judah and in the streets of Jerusalem; and they became a waste and a desolation, as they still are today. (Jer. 44:5–6)

Biblical scholar Walter Brueggemann sees punishment for disobedience as the working out of contractual theology. He perceives God's anger in the Hebrew Bible as part of what he calls the common contractual theology of disobedience and judgment. Brueggemann insists that contractual theology must be seen in tension with the Hebrew protest against it, as illustrated in the book of Job.

Repeatedly called "blameless and upright," Job suffers a series of devastating losses: his children, his animals, finally his health. Job stands by his own integrity: he has done nothing to deserve such treatment. He also refuses to curse God. The drama of Job is a challenge to the theology of disobedience and judgment. Ultimately, God accepts Job's persistent complaint and restores Job's fortunes. God transcends contractual theology. (Never mind that sons and daughters lost their lives in the process. Never mind what happened to the mothers of seven sons and three daughters.)

The message of Job is that contractual theology is an inadequate formula for explaining suffering and loss. Human attempts to assign divine motivation to pain, failure, and punishment are wrongheaded.

While the dominant mode of Hebrew Bible theology is contractual, a countertheme of protest is in tension with contractual theology.[12] People hurt, protest, and no matter the struggle, they continue to hope in God's goodness and love. Hurt and hope, Brueggemann believes, provide a major theme of the Hebrew Bible. Everywhere in the biblical narrative people hurt, and people hope in God's promise that God cares and that God seeks justice. Brueggemann sees the experience of pain and the liberation from it as "the main question of Old Testament faith." He writes:

> By *embrace of pain* is meant the full acknowledgment of and experience of pain and the capacity and willingness to make that pain a substantive part of Israel's faith-conversation with its God. Such an act of embrace means to articulate the pain fully, to insist on God's reception of the speech and the pain, and to wait hopefully for God's resolution. The term "pain" here refers to any dysfunction in the relationship with God and to any derivative dysfunction in the disorder of creation or society.[13]

Brueggemann sees the embrace of pain as an active facing of the pain, refusing to submerge it and instead forcing it onto God's agenda. Nonetheless, I struggle with the concept of embracing pain, lest it convey the message that persons ought to suffer, if not willingly, too patiently. My fear is that the protest may be lost in the embrace. Too many women have been advised to embrace pain in a passive way, to accept abusive institutions or abusive relationships as their challenge or cross to bear. I prefer using the language *pain resistance*.

Resisting disorder of creation or society includes an articulation of the pain—fully, frequently, and with a loud voice. All oppressed people of faith can pray the lament psalms as part of their private and public outcry against personal and social injustice, trivialization, and abuse.

While once I might have said that the next step is to wait hopefully for God's resolution, now I want all people who are abused to persist in resisting pain with the faith that God is already in the struggle. I realize that trusting that God is in the struggle can be almost impossible in the midst of abuse. If the abused person is able to cling to such faith, then the process will involve both restless agitating and hopeful, but not passive, waiting.

My appropriation of the Brueggemann statement quoted above is that *resistance to pain* means the full acknowledgment and experience of pain and the capacity and willingness to make that pain a substantive part of one's faith conversation with God. Such an act of resistance means to articulate the pain fully, to insist on God's reception of the speech and the pain, and to persist in resisting pain with the faith assurance that God is already in the struggle of resistance. Both restless agitating and hopeful expectation of God's resolution continue until one experiences concrete change.

In the last analysis, Brueggemann's helpful words about Yahweh's anger are not primarily about Yahweh. They are about the biblical writers' deepest convictions about Yahweh, and they are about human disappointment, anger, and hope. The biblical writers are engaged in a struggle with injustice and bring God into the conversation. Holding neither that texts are human creations nor that they speak the mind of God, Brueggemann believes that "the biblical artists enter into the struggle in which God is involved."[14]

Covenantal or contractual theology comes under serious critique, however, in David Blumenthal's theology of protest. Covenantal theology is indeed two-sided: "As God is angry with us in covenant, so we are angry with [God] in covenant." Rage is transformed into righteous anger, into a moral claim against God, expressed in cries for vindication. The problem Blumenthal sees is that the cries become fantasy:

> The suffering is real. . . . But the appeal to Big Papa to come and gore our enemies is pure fantasy . . . a projection of our own impotence in the face of ego-destroying power. . . . Better to rage authentically than to transubstantiate into fantasy. A curse upon fantasy, for it cripples us, castrates us, and renders

us impotent! In the hierarchy of power relations, only transgression through self-determination saves, or at least comforts.[15]

This challenge has more to do with the expression of human anger than with the anger of God. (Blumenthal's understanding of human rage is dealt with in the discussion of a theology of human anger.)

So far I have considered three possible interpretations of God's anger: God is abusive; God's anger is in tension with God's love; God's anger is a response to the breaking of covenant with God. Might it be that God's anger in the Bible is more projection on the part of humankind than descriptive of God? I turn to a fourth interpretation of divine wrath: God's anger is a projection of the human search for meaning.

Interpretation 4.
The Biblical Account of a Wrathful God Is a Human Attempt to Find Meaning in the Midst of Chaos and Loss

How easy it is for people to assign a cause or blame someone when tragedy comes their way. (The socialization of women and men makes it far more likely for a woman to assume she is at fault and for a man to find something or someone outside of himself to blame.[16] In either case, the need seems to be to assign a cause that accounts for the effect.) Then the event makes enough rational sense that the one in pain can either be resigned to it or have another to blame. Often enough, people of faith assume that God is punishing them for breaking covenant. At least the question "Why me?" can be answered.[17]

I return to the drama of Job. One way to read the book of Job is to experience it as a dramatic presentation on the theme of loss and tragedy. Job cannot apply the biblical law of "eye for eye, tooth for tooth" (Deut. 19:21; Ex. 21:24) to his massive misfortune. He is blameless and upright. How, then, to find meaning in the midst of chaos and loss? Job cries out that God is directly responsible for his loss of children, possessions, and health:

> He has torn me in his wrath, and hated me; he has gnashed his teeth at me; my adversary sharpens his eyes against me. . . . I was at ease, and he broke me in two; he seized me by the neck and dashed me to pieces; he set me up as his target. . . . He bursts upon me again and again; he rushes at me like a warrior. (Job 16:9,12,14)

The biblical text offers a glimpse of the human struggle to believe in a God above chaos, a God who can bring meaning out of tragedy. Job is anything but patient in his suffering. His is the story of one particular person's struggle with loss in life and his subsequent crisis of faith in God; it is also about God's responsiveness to human rage.

Meaning in the chaos comes to Job just before he has his fortune restored. In the last chapter of the drama, Job recognizes that, after all, he is not blameless. When he has found his meaning, that is, when he has seen God, he recognizes himself: "Therefore I despise myself, and repent in dust and ashes" (42:6). Job is no longer in chaos.

The book of Job proclaims that cause cannot be assigned to much of the tragedy in life. God did not "do it." Human beings may not "deserve it." No rational explanation exists. In the process of finding meaning in the midst of loss, Job speculated that a wrathful God was the cause of his distress.

If God's wrath is not the cause of human suffering, then might God's wrath be nothing more than a projection of human wrath?

Interpretation 5.
God's Wrath Is a Projection
of Humankind's Wrath

One might claim that the scriptural passages depicting an angry God are primitive expressions of humankind's destructive rage. As the earlier chapters of this book have demonstrated, anger is a difficult, disturbing emotion. Few people know how to use it well.

Unable to channel their rage constructively, the biblical writers displaced human anger onto God. Angry at themselves, angry at people or institutions in their lives, they imagined God as the angry one. Angry enough to destroy those perceived as enemies, they asked God to be the agent of annihilation: "Let ruin come on them unawares" (Ps. 35:8); "[God] will repay my enemies for their evil . . . put an end to them" (Ps. 54:5). While the psalmist may recognize human evil—"Wash me thoroughly from my iniquity, and cleanse me from my sin" (Ps. 51:2)—the plea is always for God's blessing on the one who prays and God's curse on the enemy.

As discussed previously, anger shows up in the early months of life when infants' needs are not satisfied. Toddlers will strike out at one another when their desires are frustrated. Throughout the life cycle the struggle continues as people face frustration and unmet wants and needs, pain, and violent abuse. They become enraged and curse within their hearts, if not in spoken words. Yet their fantasy tells them that willfulness and evil thoughts will be punished. They strike out in retaliation and fear the consequences. Angry, guilty, fearful people project the underside of human life onto the All Powerful, the one with the last word who will find satisfaction through some form of punishment.

The angry God takes God's vengeance. When faced with human tragedy, many people interpret painful experiences as divine punishment: "My child died in an accident because many years ago I . . ." This is God portrayed in the image of humankind. When human beings cannot forgive themselves, they often project vengeance onto an angry God. The psalmist prays:

> You have put me in the depths of the Pit,
> in the regions dark and deep.
> Your wrath lies heavy upon me,
> and you overwhelm me with all your waves.
> . . . .
> Your wrath has swept over me;
> your dread assaults destroy me.
>   (Ps. 88:6–7, 16)

A sense of divine punishment is heard in the parable of the faithful and the unfaithful servant. Jesus is reported to have said of the wicked servant, "The master of that slave will come on a day when he does not expect him and at an hour that he does not know. He will cut him in pieces and put him with the hypocrites, where there will be weeping and gnashing of teeth" (Matt. 24:50–51).

Human beings search for reasons why they suffer; they also project their wrath onto the all-powerful Other. The fourth and fifth interpretations of the wrath of God in the Bible suggest that God's wrath is really human projection—a search for meaning in the midst of chaos and loss, and an attempt to distance oneself from human anger and rage.

I come to one final interpretation, the one with which I live: there is no adequate interpretation of God's wrath, save to say that everything about God is mysterious to humankind.

Interpretation 6.
God's Anger Is a Mystery,
Beyond Rational Explanation

Because God is the infinite Other and because human beings are finite, God's anger will never be fully understood. God's nature and human nature make such understanding impossible. God's anger is as mysterious as God's knowledge and power and love. *Human beings cannot know God's inner life.* One can know how persons believed to have been inspired, beginning with the biblical writers, reveal God as one who loves justice and hates sin. God's anger is related to the love of justice and the hatred of sin.

Speaking in God's name, the biblical writers too have loved justice and hated sin. In making sense of the pain and suffering in life, as well as the wonder and ecstasy, one also knows her or his own experience of God. And one can know how persons of all times who have seemingly lived their lives centered in God and in the things of God have spoken of God.

Yet, ultimately, the wrath of God is a mystery beyond knowing. The heart of the biblical message is that God is always with God's creation, which God sees as very good. When people fail to live God's love within their community, God must experience something analogous to human disappointment and anger. To put it more accurately, when human beings are disappointed, hurt, and angry over injustice in their world, they experience something analogous to what God experiences as God continues to be with creation in its brokenness.

Biblical accounts of God's wrath are human attempts to explain God's engagement in evil and pain and death. Nonetheless, God is revealed through those inspired attempts. The biblical God is not indifferent to what people do to one another. God takes sin seriously, hears the cry of the oppressed, and moves within the minds and hearts of people to work for the liberation of the suffering. The writers of the biblical library are convinced that God has a great vision for the human family. That hope runs far beyond faltering attempts humankind has made at building healthy, holy community.

James Whitehead and Evelyn Whitehead summarize the passion of God in scripture this way:

> The Jewish and Christian Scriptures show us a God immersed in all the passions that accompany commitment. The revelation seems to be that passions are the price of love; to be entwined in others' lives is to court sorrow as well as delight, to taste loneliness as well as communion, to come to grief as well as to gratitude.[18]

Does Jesus the Christ, revelation of God, make the mystery of God's anger more concrete? That is the question addressed in chapter 5.

5

Jesus' Anger

Who do you say that I am?
            Mark 8:29

At a local Women-Church gathering on Super Bowl Sunday (the group meets every third Sunday and always on Super Bowl Sunday), twelve women spoke of many issues relative to their history as a worshiping community, among them current beliefs or convictions regarding Jesus Christ.

Most indicated that they no longer expressed faith in God through faith in Jesus Christ and that neither Christology nor the Bible held great interest for them. While not all were ready to articulate their positions, they did not feel pressured to be clear about their beliefs—putting Jesus on hold was seen as unproblematic. What they could say with clarity was that they were in a spiritual and faith transition and that within the group they felt accepted, respected, and able to let their expressions of faith evolve. Many had been and some still are affiliated with Roman Catholic religious orders. I expressed a minority opinion, claiming renewed interest in Christology and, especially through my research on anger, a fresh motivation to read and pray the Gospels and the psalms of lament.

Later that night, I awakened from a significant dream and scribbled details that would allow me to rise in the morning to the dream's promises and possibilities. In the dream the conversation of the evening continued. Women who had gathered for worship were discussing Christology. As part of the liturgy within the dream, each woman spent reflective time on her own in various places around the home where we met.

In a meditation within the dream, I imagined Jesus having a conversation with the women who belonged to his circle of followers. The dominant message in the dream was that Jesus and I needed further conversation. The dream included an agreement that for the purpose of my book on anger, as well as for furthering the Women-Church discussion, I would add an imaginary story to the Gospel account. The narrative would take the form of a conversation between Jesus and his female disciples.

Still within the dream, I reported my meditation to the circle of women. One of the women became excited and encouraged me to write the book. What follows is a waking continuation of the challenge I accepted in the dream.

A Waking Dream

Jesus went down to the river where women from the community had gathered to wash their bundles of garments. Congregating at the river had become a regular weekly event, with newcomers joining the group from time to time. Today there was Miriam, wife of Simon, who came with her mother-in-law, Ruth. Ruth sat on a large rock from which she watched the younger women at work. Mary and Martha were there; so were Mary the mother of James, Salome, and Mary Magdalene. Myra, the Syrophoenician woman whose daughter Jesus had cured, was joining the group for the first time.

The women were in high spirits. Having a new woman join the circle always added energy and enthusiasm to their gathering. Old-timers rose to the occasion to make their time together most engaging, in hopes that the visitor would want to return. This morning they shared stories about how their week had gone, then became more serious and talked of their hopes for the community. They joked, too, about some men's reactions to their new behaviors.

Just as Jesus approached, some of the women with children were talking excitedly about how the children were making friends among themselves and even showing concern for one another, as well as a sense of being part of the community that assembled around Jesus. One reported that her daughter was using the word *we* in telling a friend about the discussion that took place at her family home two nights before, sparking for the mother a profound moment of recognition: the movement would go on, generation to generation.

The women spoke also of their new confidence in their roles—sharing responsibility for the community through speaking to other women about God's action in their lives. The married women in their group es-

pecially wanted women in the villages to know that increasingly their husbands saw them as individuals with their own hopes and dreams. They
were convinced that men were increasingly influenced by the respect
Jesus showed the women. Others were afraid that their new indepen-
dence would create unbearable conflict in their marriages.

At first, Jesus leaned against the rock where Miriam sat. He appeared
to be lost in thought and at the same time seemed reluctant to intrude in
the conversation. Once he was noticed by the women, however, the ani-
mated talk at the edge of the river subsided, and they turned their attention to Jesus. Men did not usually come down to the river's edge when the
women took care of the washing; Jesus' presence made them self-
conscious and also both puzzled and delighted them.

Jesus took off his sandals and waded into the shallow water. The
ensuing conversation went something like this:

JESUS: I have been thinking of you all morning, and your conversation increases my concern. What saddens me is a fear that one day you will
question whether you can follow me. You will feel the need to walk
away from the community because I am a man.

WOMAN: What do you mean? Why would we reject a man? Where
would that leave us? So much of our life is controlled by men that
we would have nothing without them. What you're saying makes
no sense.

JESUS: I'm afraid that men will use the fact that I am a man to perpetuate
power over you. They will not accept the leadership of women.
Already some religious leaders rumble about my relationship with
you.

WOMAN: Tell us what you hear. We have just been talking about how some
of our partners pick up your positive attitudes toward us as your
equal, and others seem threatened.

JESUS: Well, take Myra for example. A local leader just asked me how I
could transgress customs by attending to a Syrophoenician woman.
What they don't understand is that Myra helped me see that my attention to the Jews was in conflict with what I preach about God's
love being for all people. I was wrong to call her people "dogs."

WOMAN: But if you keep doing these wonderful things, treating us as
equals and changing customs, surely some of the threatened men will
begin to understand.

JESUS: Perhaps. I don't think I have enough time to make a great enough
difference. Anyway, this morning I was thinking about you women
and needed to come down and join you. If men continue to dominate

you, and at the same time you know that in God's eyes men and women are equal partners, then you will be angry that your religion oppresses women. I fear for what will come of the movement we are beginning.

WOMAN: The more self-confident we become, the more we can effect change. Men will *have to* recognize our leadership.

JESUS: I'm afraid that change will not come easily. Who knows? The authorities may use the fact that I am a man to say that God's plan is that men rule over women.

You will surely question whether I can be the revelation of God for you—whether my being a man suggests that in God's eyes women are second to men.

This is hard for me to put into simple words, but I wonder if, after I'm gone, the focus will shift from the message about God's love for all and our work for justice and real community to an abstract concern over how as a man I am one with God.

WOMAN: We don't understand what you are saying. Would you have to be a woman for us? Or would there have to be two of you claiming to speak for God?

The conversation ended. The dream underscored the struggle I have been in for years—no, it did much more than that. The dream helped me find Jesus in that struggle. He made it his own. The dream brought home to me that my faith in the Jesus movement lives; it also brought home the sadness and loss I feel when I am among women who no longer call themselves Christian. The dream gave me a glimpse of the anger the risen Christ must experience at the profound injustice toward women that has been perpetrated in the churches founded in God's name simply because Jesus was male.

I write these lines during the week after Pope John Paul II's most recent proclamation, a reiteration of many of his statements, that there will never be women priests in the Roman Catholic Church, a decision he bases on the fact that Jesus called only male disciples. The anger I felt when I heard that news turned to laughter as I read Garry Wills's response in the *Washington Post*. Wills suggests that the pope apply his principle with far greater rigor: male priests, like the twelve apostles called by Jesus, must be married, Greek-speaking Jews, and they need not write at all.[1]

While Wills's perspective dispelled my immediate rage, I remain aware that the pope's proclamation has aggravated for many women the perception of a great distance between themselves and the male figure of Jesus. Yet I do not believe that this distance, which has been widened throughout history by policies and interpretations hostile to women taking leadership roles in the church, is a divide either made by God or sanctioned by Jesus. My dream provided me, on the contrary, with a glimpse of Jesus' anger at this division. What more can be learned about Jesus' anger?

People who have been steeped in Christian experience do not start out to explore the anger of Jesus in the Bible the same way they might explore, for example, the anger of Mary Magdalene or Peter or Paul. Christians bring claims about Jesus to their reading. Not only do they bring faith claims to the texts, but the central foci of the Gospels themselves are claims about the man from Nazareth. The nature of those claims undoubtedly will shape one's reading of the Bible.

My struggle with a theology of anger has pushed me to revisit the question Jesus asked of a disciple and to hear it once again asked of me: Who do you say that I am? It is only after answering the question that I explore the anger of Jesus in the Bible.

The Christological Question
Revisited

How many sermons, how many conferences, how many articles have repeated the question that Mark[2] has Jesus ask of Peter at the center of the Gospel, "Who do you say that I am?"[3] All four of the Gospels are centrally concerned with the identity of this man, which allows many Gospel readers to come up with short, clear answers to the key question: Jesus is God. Jesus is Lord. Jesus is the Son of God, the Son of man, the Messiah. The following answer is not short; my effort has been to gain clarity.

Who do you say that I am? In Mark's account of the baptism of Jesus, a voice from heaven proclaims that Jesus is the beloved Son, on whom God's favor rests (Mark 1:10–11). While God recognizes the person and mission of Jesus, Jesus repeatedly in the first half of the Gospel instructs people who walk with him not to tell what they know about his identity and destiny. The unclean spirits recognize him, yet the disciples are not to reveal who Jesus is: "Whenever the unclean spirits saw him, they fell down before him and shouted, 'You are the Son of God!' But he sternly ordered them not to make him known" (3:11–12).

Silencing by Jesus constitutes Mark's messianic secret, a theme that keeps the question of Jesus' identity open from the beginning to the end of the Gospel. The secret, ironically, is only within the Gospel. While the characters in the book are not to know, the readers do know the secret: Jesus is the Messiah.

Here, at the center of the book, almost as if Jesus were leading the first Christology seminar while traveling along the road to Caesarea Philippi, he seems to want his disciples to recognize him. "Who do you say that I am?" It appears that he is seeking not public recognition but personal confession through a full and intentional working relationship to him as one who speaks and acts in God's name. "Recognize who I am and what I am about, so that you can truly be with me in my work" is implied in the text. Jesus seems to be in search of a shared ministry: namely, a ministry of making incarnate the good news that God is truly with humankind.

The question put to Peter follows the story of the blind man who, on having his sight restored, saw people first as walking trees, then clearly. With caution, this can be read as something of a mini-stage theory of human faith. Caution is in order because the metaphor is not intended to place less value on persons who are physically blind or to suggest that their physical blindness indicates anything about their spiritual or moral condition. Rather, the metaphor suggests that sometimes people are unable to sense the sacred dimension of human life. Sometimes their understanding is distorted; sometimes they comprehend clearly. The passage after the question put to Peter is the story of the transfiguration, another passage to which vision is essential—as is hearing. Having seen Jesus bathed in dazzling light and in conversation with Elijah and Moses, the disciples hear a heavenly voice echoing the voice heard at the baptism: this person is mine; listen to him.

Near the end of the Gospel, Jesus himself answers questions about his identity raised by the high priest: "Are you the Messiah, the Son of the Blessed One?" (14:61). Jesus acknowledges that he is. The high priest and, later, Pilate do not recognize him as the Messiah. It is finally the centurion, watching Jesus die, who admits the truth and reveals the secret: "Truly this man was God's Son!" (15:39).

Why is the question of Jesus' identity so important? I have heard feminist friends ask, "Who cares?" when the question of Jesus' nature is raised. Because the maleness of Jesus has been used by some denominations to exclude women from full partnership in the work of the church, many women have painfully walked away, often full of anger and sadness. Others have happily run away from what they consider to be a patriarchal institution beyond redemption.

Still other women and men who move away from traditional Christology do so because they think the claims have proven themselves invalid. For example, a male colleague who describes himself as post-Christian repeatedly argues that if Jesus was the Messiah, sent to initiate a new kingdom of justice, and if all of the millions of the world's baptized are new beings in Christ, why is the world such a wretched place for the majority of humankind? Why has the program failed so miserably?

Undoubtedly because my life has been profoundly marked by faith in Jesus of Nazareth, the person and his message, I can neither walk nor run. I return to the question, each time from a new perspective, and hear it asked of me: Who do you say that I am? Surely one's reply will affirm, alter, or deny a particular expression of faith. Not only is the symbolic world that shapes my religious and spiritual life marked by my reply; my understanding of how I am called by God to live is made concrete by my answer.[4] My conviction is that the answer, in addition to invigorating one's spiritual life, will also help a person come to terms with her or his anger.

Who, then, is Jesus? Jesus, born of Mary, is one sent by God to reveal who God is. At the same time, Jesus reveals what it is to be human. Specifically, Jesus revealed what it is to be *man*. Jesus broke the old mold and cast a new one for males. He was servant. He ate with sinners. He spoke with women in public. He put people above the law. He invited women into his circle of leaders.

Jesus had a thorough awareness of the pervasive presence and power of God in human life. Unlike the church established in his name, he did not focus on himself. He focused on the Holy One. His parables and brief sayings, which scholars say come closest to the words Jesus would actually have used, focus on God's intention for human community.

God wants an intimate, familial relationship with each person. Jesus addresses the Holy One as Abba to make that point (Mark 14:36). In a Jewish community in which people did not call on God by name, Jesus' use of an everyday, warm, affectionate title that translates as "Daddy" or "Papa" (more appropriately than "Father") may have come as a shock to his listeners. God is as close as your central familial people. Would that he had also used the term for Mama, so that patriarchal churches would have to give up their excessive, idolatrous use of male language in describing the Holy One.

Abba, however, as feminist theologian Rosemary Ruether reminds us, speaks of more than familiarity. Calling the Holy One "Abba" says that humankind has but one father or patriarch. who replaces the hierarchical, patriarchal family with a community of equal brothers and sisters.[5] In other words, the Gospels challenged the role of family in the culture of their time. No longer was a person to seek her or his security and honor in the household into which she or he is born. No longer would a person be shamed because her or his family lacked power and prestige. While one rightly seeks affection and support from one's given family, the locus of security and identity is the new family of Abba. To be a member of the new household is to live under one Abba, to be a part of a community that constitutes a new family.

To balance the male language that permeates the Christian churches, feminist theologian Rita Nakashima Brock uses a female form of the word *Christ* and calls the new family of believers *Christa community*.[6] *Christa* signals that women are equal members of the body of Christ.

Whereas the Acts of the Apostles may idealize the early Christian community, the evidence the book gives is that concern for the establishment of a caring community was at the forefront of the church:

> All who believed were together and had all things in common; they would sell their possessions and goods and distribute the proceeds to all, as any had need. Day by day, as they spent much time together in the temple, they broke bread at home and ate their food with glad and generous hearts, praising God and having the goodwill of all the people. (Acts 2:44–47)

The message is simple: love and respect for self and neighbor and God, a message that thrives in Christian base communities, in Women-Church groups around the world, and, it is hoped, in many local congregations as well.

Through the epistles attributed to Paul, however, the early church was also instructed to subordinate women to men, wives to husbands, and to keep women silent in the churches (1 Cor. 11:3–9; 14:34–36). The more egalitarian community of the early church soon was replaced by a hierarchy of patriarchal power.[7] The focus on God-centered community initiated by a leader named Jesus, who pointed followers toward the mystery of an indwelling God, shifted as the community became structured and controlled by men. The leadership of the established church echoed the patriarchal hierarchy of the world in which it was embedded. Jesus Christ himself, rather than the God Jesus revealed, became the focus of Christian religion and the center of worship.[8]

While patriarchal themes were present before the fourth century, Nicean Christology fused messianic expectations with the suffering-servant imagery of Isaiah, at the same time integrating the cosmological ideas of *sophia* and *logos*.[9] Jesus is Messiah, the promised one. Jesus is the suffering servant. Jesus is the Sophia, or wisdom of God. Jesus is the Word of God spoken from the beginning. Jesus is the ruler of the universe, coming to judge the living and the dead. Jesus is King of kings and Lord of lords. Needless to say, kings and lords are male; Sophia isn't! (Sophia/Wisdom has been lost so completely from the tradition that when women, in their efforts to reimagine the symbols of their faith, bring this name for God back into their worship circles, members of the churches and their judicatories become enraged. Witness the enormous cries of protest, accompanied by threats as well as punishment, that have followed the 1993 Re-Imagining Conference.)

While in the earliest years of the church both men and women had been encouraged to teach and prophesy, long before the fourth century the imperial church had thoroughly reinstated hierarchy and validated radical patriarchy. The consolidation of church and state happened at many levels. The Edict of Milan (316 C.E.) provided for the legal toleration of Christianity. In the second through the fourth decades of the fourth century, the state granted moneys for clergy and Christian buildings. Finally, through the bishops of the church, there was direct imperial intervention in church affairs, as illustrated when Emperor Constantine called the first council of bishops in 325 to settle the Arian controversy over the relationship between the Father and the Logos.[10] Eusebius of Nicomedia, spokesperson for Arius, not only was shouted down and had his speech snatched from his hands, torn to shreds, and trampled on but was declared a heretic and deposed. After winning the support of his distant relative, Constantine, Eusebius convinced the emperor that he had been treated too harshly. Under order from Constantine, the bishop of Constantinople restored Eusebius of Nicomedia to communion.[11]

The church used state-backed power to enforce patriarchy as the only pattern permitted. From home to church to state, women were subordinated and punished. The discipleship of equals was lost; women's roles in the movement were eliminated.[12] With the first three chapters of Genesis cited by male leaders as evidence of women's inferiority, women were put in their place: man, mate; woman, helpmate. The good news was that women could be saved by childbearing:

> Let a woman learn in silence with full submission. I permit no woman to teach or to have authority over a man; she is to keep silent. For Adam was formed first, then Eve; and Adam was not deceived, but the woman was deceived and became a transgressor. Yet she will be saved through childbearing, provided they continue in faith and love and holiness, with modesty. (1 Tim. 2:11–15)

God was male; the Logos (severed from its Sophia roots), son. Only men had perfect humanity, and only men could represent God, a distortion of the message of the biblical Jesus still enforced by law in Roman Catholicism and the Eastern Orthodox Church and enforced by practice in many denominations.

More disturbing still is that the emperor was believed by some to embody Christ, the ruler of all:

> Among those who conceive a direct relation between human history and the second coming of our Lord, various Fathers of the first three centuries, and Hippolytus in particular, devoted much effort to speculations upon the "weeks of the years" in the book of Daniel, or upon the seven millennia, with a view to dating the end of the world. Others worked out a system based on the succession of empires. Eusebius [of Caesarea] founded the theology of history upon the providential coincidence of Christian monotheism and Constantinian monarchy.[13]

Thus developed the image of Christ the cosmic ruler, the cosmic principle of all hierarchy, with countless little rulers at the top of countless little hierarchies. Whether emperor or pope, for one man to be seen as the ruler or the special embodiment of divinity is a setup for the abuse of others, and particularly of women.

While women in the church were subordinate to a male hierarchy and a male clergy, there was an area wherein women were able to exercise power and control over their own lives, although such freedom lasted only from the seventh to the tenth centuries. The founders and abbesses of religious communities of women enjoyed power reserved for bishops, abbots, and ordained clergy. In general, women who chose the convent were freer to use their intellectual and spiritual capacities than those who chose marriage and family.

Convents fell prey, however, to the centralizing tendencies of the eleventh, twelfth, and thirteenth centuries. Religious orders of women came under the direct supervision of male ecclesiastics. Women were no longer to have final say in the management of property. Emperor Charlemagne upheld the authority of bishops over abbesses; he even refused women the liberty of assisting in the administration of the sacraments.[14]

What somehow remains hidden to some men is that Christology has been used to affirm the ascendancy of man over woman. To assume any male privilege because of the sex of Jesus is a tragic distortion of the gospel message. Equally problematic are Christologies that affirm the divinity of Jesus over his humanity, which is to deny the radical nature of the incarnation. What too easily follows is the assumption that followers of Jesus are to transcend their humanity. The divine Jesus Christ, beyond human frailty, is far removed from the prophetic fisherman who wandered the shores of the Sea of Galilee seeking a revolution of values.

When almost exclusively male images are used to name the holy, a further assumption is made identifying what is divine with what is male and what is earthly with what is female, leading not only to the denigration of women but to the denigration of ordinary human life, especially human emotion. This makes it exceedingly difficult for Christians to recognize and enact their anger as holy energy for change. When Jesus is recognized not as God-himself-man but as God's revelation of the holiness of human life, female as well as male, women come closer to recognizing their holiness. Further, when Jesus is known as brother and leader, as the outstanding one among a community of people who were passionate about justice, both personal and social anger (his and ours) become more evident and can be more constructively expressed.

In reworking my Christology, I have often felt the obligation—sometimes because of explicit challenge by male colleagues, sometimes because of both unconscious and conscious needs—to find continuity in my faith, to bring forward the tradition; in other words, to start at Nicea and avoid heresy. Korean feminist theologian Chung Hyun Kyung gave me new incentive and new courage. I experienced what I can only describe as a delicious moment of recognition, connection, and perhaps envy when I read Kyung's description of Asian women's efforts to construct theology. She reports that Asian women have no need to defend the tradition. They do not start with dogma; they start with experience. Their experience is deeply marked by oppression; their religious task is clearly one of liberation. My agreement with her shook me to the roots as I read:

> For many Korean women, Jesus is not the objectified divine being whom people must worship. Rather, Jesus is the one we relive through our lives. The meaning of Immanuel, then, has been changed through Korean mythological symbols and language from God-*with*-us to God-*among*-us, and finally to God-*is*-us in our struggle to reclaim our full humanity.[15]

People threatened by change or particularly resistant to any alteration of dogmatic statements about Jesus Christ are quick to say that such feminist and womanist theologizing is an attempt to create God in women's own image. Far from creating anything new, believing that *God-is-us* is a radical, clear-sighted interpretation of incarnational theology. Just as Jesus might say, "If you want to know who God is, then look at me," so members of the body of Christ can echo that claim: "If you want to know where God is, then look at us."

The dramatic difference is that the gospel portrays Jesus as a man who never wavered in his resolve to be godlike. Followers of Jesus waver day in and day out. God-is-Jesus was a constant in Jesus' life. Fully human, Jesus affirmed that the very stuff of human reality is involved in the mystery of God. A human face reveals the mystery of God. This is a thoroughly sacramental understanding of one's world. To be godlike is the gospel mandate.

For some, the christological question has to do with the nature of Jesus. For others, the basic concern is the message of Jesus. Whatever Jesus is in his nature, his message is essentially a challenge: choose life— which is to love and be true to yourself and your neighbor and, through that love and fidelity, to love and be true to your God. While Jesus claimed oneness with God, nowhere did he say that believers are to assert sure knowledge about his nature in trinitarian formulas.

In a discussion with a colleague, I used the expression *low Christology*, a term that may well be too confusing to be helpful and which I no longer employ. I chose the term to disassociate myself from Christologies that become idolatries. My colleague argued for a *high Christology*, which he believed is necessary if Christians are to be secure in their belief that "all of humanity, male and female, are assumed and re-turned to the Holy One."

Sure knowledge is extremely important to many believers. High Christology helps people cope with insecurity, offering both doctrinal clarity about the nature of Jesus as well as a guaranteed place in the realm beyond this world. They need only to remain faithful.

What if I start with the premise that such security is neither part of the human condition nor what Jesus promised? What if I start with the premise that life is indeed a risk but that faith in a God who is and who cares makes it a purposeful risk? What if I believe that there was no need for Jesus to return anything to God, that God has been caught up in every part of human life from its beginning, without ceasing?

In chapter 4, I dealt briefly with theories of atonement wherein God requires or demands the sacrificial death of God's only Son for hu-mankind to be saved. Feminist and womanist theologians in particular question the need for theories of atonement based on retribution. God has never been without God's world, without God's people.

Christology that borders on idolatry has Jesus making things right for us, saving us from sin and death through submitting in obedience to God's will that he give his life for our salvation. If one believes that no God of love and justice would require blood sacrifice of a human being, then Jesus' death is seen as tragic. Jesus had to die because he was human. Jesus did not have to die the excruciating death he died, however, in order to satisfy God's need—a requirement that Joanne Carlson Brown and Rebecca Parker have called "divine child abuse."[16]

No unjust death is willed by God. Jesus did not have to be crucified to fulfill prophecy or to save us from sin. The question is not whether Jesus had to die a particular kind of death in order to satisfy God. The question is why Jesus died a torturous death at the hands of people who made themselves his enemies. And the answer is that his life and his message were a threat to the powerful.[17] Jesus died because all human beings die; in his dying, Jesus revealed the significance of living one's convictions with integrity. Or as Rita Nakashima Brock believes, Jesus did not die to save us; we are saved by God, whom we discover in the resurrection community in which we live and die. In that community, God nurtures us into our willfulness.[18]

God does not demand obedience to the authorities. God lures us into a willful seizing of every opportunity to make justice—in our relationships, in our homes, in our institutions (perhaps beginning with the church), and in our society. If God did not demand the obedience unto death on the cross of God's only son, then we do not need a theory of atonement at all. We need, perhaps, an alternative way to look at the word *atonement*, one that does not require retributive, vicarious justice. Atonement also means "to be at one with." Unfortunately, this is not the understanding of atonement most preached in the churches.

In the swirl of thought and feeling that the prophetic voices of Chung Hyun Kyung and Rita Brock triggered in my mind and heart, I faced a crippling fact: I found an embedded code in my psyche, well learned long ago. The code words are *humble obedience*. Be anything but willful. Check in with God's will, because most likely it is not your will. Replacing that code with one that says, "Have faith in yourself and don't dare give your power away," is an ongoing challenge. I experience it as a holy call.

Who, then, is Jesus? I conclude that what Jesus preached and how he lived are far more important to Christian life than are dogmatic statements about his nature. Feminist theologian Carter Heyward says it best:

> Jesus is to be remembered, not revered. Remembering Jesus does not warrant Jesusolatry or Christolatry, the idolatry of a male God. Remembering Jesus does not warrant the worshiping of Jesus, but rather must compel us to look prayerfully to the god of Jesus. The one whom Jesus called "Abba": Daddy. Moreover, to remember Jesus does not mean that we "imitate" Jesus, but rather that, like him, we seek to act with God in our own time, under the

political, social, psychological, physical, and institutional conditions of our own place.[19]

Jesus, born of Mary, is one sent by God to reveal what it is to be human. I sometimes say that Jesus is a passion, rather than saying that Jesus is a man. Jesus was passionate for justice. He was passionate about life, about community, about God. His life demonstrated what it means to belong to a human household, a community of women and men who not only take God seriously but find their identity and security through their shared faith. While the portrait that followers of Jesus have been given focuses almost exclusively on the final three years of his life, the fact that he was born of Mary is assurance that from infancy through his death, Jesus felt all of the emotions that human beings experience, anger among them. I turn now to the Gospels to explore the anger of Jesus, God-is-us.

The Anger of Jesus in the New Testament

Perhaps it is easier to speak of the anger of God, whom one does not see, than to speak of the anger of flesh-and-blood Jesus, seen through the eyes of the evangelists. Almost nothing is recorded about the life of Jesus (let alone his anger) prior to his brief public life. Most of what is known about the affective life of Jesus must be surmised from the concise, selective accounts of four evangelists, which, with the exception of John, collapse Jesus' public life into one year; the Gospel of John spans three years.[20]

For starters, one can say that as a fully human person, Jesus must have known all of the emotions and feeling states that human beings experience. A person passionate for justice, he surely must have felt frustration, anger, and sadness at the injustices he saw around him. While the Gospels apply the word *anger* to Jesus only once (when he healed a man with a withered hand), anger is written between the lines many times.

This reflection relies mostly on the Gospel of Mark, except in cases where one of the other Gospels includes a relevant incident not found in Mark. No attempt is made here of extensive biblical exegesis. Rather, my purpose is to take the story at face value, asking what Jesus might have thought and felt had events happened as recorded.

In the first chapter of the Gospel, Mark reports that immediately after his baptism by John, Jesus spent forty days in the wilderness, both tempted by Satan and attended by angels (Mark 1:12–13). Only thirty-three words in the English translation describe a forty-day period of both trial and consolation. Could anyone endure such an ordeal without recurring feelings of pain, anguish, and anger? How does anyone fight against temptation without knowing fear and anger?

In the same chapter Jesus is confronted by a man with an unclean spirit (1:23–27). Mark writes that Jesus rebuked the unclean spirit, ordered "him" out. Spirits that destroy human life must surely have stirred the anger of Jesus. *Rebuke* is a strong word, descriptive of the response of one experiencing a cluster of intense feelings, anger among them.

Mark 3 includes the single occasion when Jesus is explicitly described as angry.[21] Jesus entered the synagogue and came face to face with a man whose hand was withered. Some pharisees (no assumption that they represented all pharisees) who wanted to catch Jesus breaking the law observed the incident as it unfolded:

> They watched him to see whether he would cure him on the sabbath, so that they might accuse him. And he said to the man who had the withered hand, "Come forward." Then he said to them, "Is it lawful to do good or to do harm on the sabbath, to save life or to kill?" But they were silent. He looked around at them with anger; he was grieved at their hardness of heart and said to the man, "Stretch out your hand." He stretched it out, and his hand was restored. The Pharisees went out and immediately conspired with the Herodians against him, how to destroy him. (Mark 3:2–6)

There are two angers here. The anger that destroys is side by side with anger that works for change. Initially, a group of people who resist the message of Jesus are on watch to catch him doing something against their law. The implication is that they were angry because Jesus threatened their sense of security. Observance of the law measured worth. How could they be sure of their position if the law was not the measure? "They watched him . . . so that they might accuse him."

Mark juxtaposes this story with Jesus saying, "The sabbath was made for humankind, and not humankind for the sabbath" (2:27). Mark then has Jesus put his saying into action. First he asked those watching in judgment if the law could ever be used to prevent one from doing good. They remained silent.

The text indicates that their silence angered Jesus. What he did with his anger was reach out to heal a suffering man. In reaction to his creative use of anger, he received the anger of fear and hatred: Jesus must be destroyed. In other words, Jesus' anger at injustice is fair warning to women and men: if you express your justice-anger, then the powers-that-be may well work to destroy you with their fear-and-hatred anger.

Later in the same chapter, Mark records that the family of Jesus thought they needed to restrain him, having heard from the townsfolk that Jesus was out of his mind (3:20–22). One can imagine that Jesus was exasperated and, yes, angry to be so outrageously misunderstood. Worse still, others accused Jesus of being possessed by a demon. They confused the Holy One, in whose name Jesus responded to need, with Beelzebul, the ruler of demons. Jesus is reported to have said in rebuttal that blasphemy against the Holy Spirit is an eternal sin (Mark 3:23–30). This language is more than a rebuke; it is the response of a misunderstood, misinterpreted, very angry Jesus.

In Mark 6, Jesus returned to his hometown, Nazareth. I have tried in prayer to take this journey with Jesus. Nazareth was so familiar that Jesus knew every corner of it by heart—he had not been gone long enough for many changes to have occurred. It was as if he returned to each square of the town; he recognized almost every face.

> On the sabbath he began to teach in the synagogue, and many who heard him were astounded. They said, "Where did this man get all this? What is this wisdom that has been given to him? What deeds of power are being done by his hands! Is not this the carpenter, the son of Mary and brother of James and Joses and Judas and Simon, and are not his sisters here with us?" And they took offense at him. Then Jesus said to them, "Prophets are not without honor, except in their hometown, and among their own kin, and in their own house." And he could do no deed of power there, except that he laid his hands on a few sick people and cured them. And he was amazed at their unbelief. (Mark 6:2–6)

Backs turned on him. Some rejected him to his face. Others murmured among themselves, too fearful to speak directly to him. What feelings clustered with Jesus' amazement? Is it possible to be rejected by people who are one's roots without feeling profound disappointment, alienation, hurt, and anger?

In the same chapter, Mark records the irrational, gruesome death of John the Baptist, beheaded at Herod's orders on Herod's birthday, at the request of the daughter of his wife, Herodias. The disciples took the body and buried it. In his Gospel, Matthew adds, "Then they went and told Jesus. Now when Jesus heard this, he withdrew from there in a boat to a deserted place by himself" (Matt. 14:12–13).

How did Jesus deal with this unspeakable tragedy? What sadness and rage must have filled his heart in learning that a God-focused messenger of such integrity and courage, a friend so close to Jesus in spirit, so filled with vision, had been senselessly, obscenely murdered. Did Jesus,

shocked and distressed and alone, battle with feelings of hatred and revenge? Surely he was filled with grief; perhaps he suffered what clinicians
would diagnose as depression. How difficult it must have been for him to
return to his ministry after such a tragic loss.

He did return, and he continued his struggle with those who resisted
the religious reforms he preached. There are several passages where Jesus
is tested by leaders of the synagogue who challenge his authority. Mark
records that on one such occasion, Jesus was asked for a sign from
heaven to support his claim to speak and act in God's name. "And he
sighed deeply in his spirit and said, 'Why does this generation ask for a
sign? Truly I tell you, no sign will be given to this generation.' And he left
them, and getting into the boat again, he went across to the other side"
(Mark 8:12; see also 11:27–33).

A deep sigh, a question apparently asked in frustration, a denial, an
exit—I find not only anger in the Markan passage but also a viable option
for dealing with anger. According to the text, Jesus did not argue, did not
give a rebuke. He simply ended the conversation and withdrew, as if to
say that sometimes when people are not ready or willing to understand,
the only protest is silence and withdrawal.

Mark says that Jesus began to talk about his suffering and death.
Peter rebuked him. Jesus responded with his own impassioned rebuke:
"Get behind me, Satan!" (8:33). A tone of anger continues as the Markan
Jesus speaks further about suffering and death, concluding, "Those who
are ashamed of me and of my words in this adulterous and sinful generation, of them the Son of Man will also be ashamed when he comes in the
glory of his Father with the holy angels" (8:38).

What feelings cluster with the awareness that others are ashamed of
you? If anger is a response to the experience of being ignored, injured,
trivialized, or rejected, then Jesus was surely angry when he concluded
that persons important to him were ashamed of him.

In the following chapter, Jesus is asked to cast out an evil spirit from
a boy whom the disciples were unable to help. The tone of the recorded
answer is one of frustration and anger, near desperation, as if Jesus had
been pushed to the point of wanting to give up on the disciples: "You
faithless generation, how much longer must I be among you? How much
longer must I put up with you?" (Mark 9:19).

In Mark's account the Temple cleansing comes between the cursing
of the fig tree and a return to the same fig tree on the following morning
(11:11–24). Both the commotion in the Temple and the cursing of the fig
tree are symbolic, prophetic actions.[22] The fig tree, symbol of peace,

security, and prosperity, which scripture scholars believe in some cases symbolizes the nation itself, is judged worthless. The Temple, "symbolic center of the Jewish social order," is deemed corrupt.[23]

Jesus, the angry prophet, curses the fig tree and drives profiteers from the Temple. One scholar suggests that Mark's account "dramatically indicated that the expected fruitfulness associated with [the Temple] is not to be true. Its destiny is rather to be withered [to the roots]!"[24] Another possible reading is that the Temple would survive its current abuse and continue to be the powerful symbol of God's faithful presence.[25] The Temple incident itself, recorded in all four Gospels, has become paradigmatic, offering a rare glimpse of Jesus caught up in powerful emotion.

There are indications of the anger of Jesus found in the other Gospel accounts but missing from Mark. When warned that Herod wants to kill him, Luke says that Jesus labeled Herod a fox, in what reads like a flash of anger (Luke 13:32–35). Accused of alignment with Beelzebul, the Matthean Jesus called his accusers a "brood of vipers," evil people who speak carelessly and will be condemned (Matt. 12:33–36). Also in Matthew, Jesus denounced persons who exalt themselves, following his denunciation with a series of woes addressed at those who offer false leadership (Matthew 23).

In the Fourth Gospel, the evangelist portrays Jesus in confrontations peppered with anger. In discussing with disciples whether their being descendants of Abraham made them slaves or free, Jesus said, "Why do you not understand what I say? . . . The reason you do not hear [the words of God] is that you are not from God" (John 8:43, 47). He goes on to call his listeners liars, an accusation one would most often make in the heat of anger (John 8:55).

Finally, the intense emotions of Jesus are seen in the passion narratives, which constitute a significant portion of each of the Gospels. Following the emphases of the different evangelists, each account of Jesus' betrayal, agony, and crucifixion varies in feeling tone. Taken separately, they throw light on the complex, intense emotions Jesus experienced during his last two days of human life.

Mark's account most reveals the struggle and pain of Jesus. At the Passover meal Jesus announced that one of his chosen, seated at the table, would betray him. After offering the bread and wine, symbols of the gift of his life, Jesus again made a grim prediction: "You will all become deserters" (14:27). Peter would deny his teacher and friend three times. When Jesus and the disciples arrived at Gethsemane, his emotions quickened. Mark describes Jesus as distressed, agitated, deeply grieved, and utterly alone. While anger undoubtedly clustered with his mix of emotions, Jesus appears to have been in a state of resignation and deep sorrow: "Have you come out with swords and clubs to arrest me as though I were a bandit?" (14:48).

Before the high priests, Jesus heard false testimony, listened to the whole assembly cry out in condemnation and ask that he be put to death. Spittle, blows, and heavy beatings followed, then a night of agony before the torturous ordeal ending in crucifixion. A cluster of experiences laden with feelings are in the account: excruciating pain, humiliation, rejection, profound disappointment, the ultimate loss of life. Was anger a part of Jesus' agony, or had he moved beyond anger to depression or resignation?

Hope battled with despair when Jesus searched for God's presence in the very last minutes of his life. Jesus' final words in Mark's story echo the distressed cry of the psalmist: "My God, my God, why have you forsaken me?" (15:34). Did Jesus continue the psalm as he died on the cross?

> Why are you so far from helping me, from the words of my groaning?
> O my God, I cry by day, but you do not answer;
> and by night, but find no rest.
> . . . .
> I am a worm, and not human;
> scorned by others and despised by the people.
> All who seek me mock at me;
> they make mouths at me, they shake their heads;
> "Commit your cause to the Lord; let him deliver—
> let him rescue the one in whom he delights!"
>
> (Ps. 22:1–2, 6–8)

Alastair Campbell notes that

> it is important to remember the lack of tranquility in Jesus when he faces his testing times. . . . We find in Jesus a real battle between hope and despair, a struggle with which we can identify because it reflects our own reactions to loss, when we will allow ourselves to feel the intensity of the pain without the anodyne of a false religion.[26]

In contrast to the struggle and betrayal of the Markan account, in the Gospels of Matthew and Luke, the Passover meal begins with Jesus predicting the banquet in the kingdom. In Luke, Jesus is strengthened by the appearance of an angel on the Mount of Olives; at the same time, he sweats drops of blood (Luke 22:43–44). Further, as he is crucified, Jesus assures the criminal hanging from his own cross, who proclaims Jesus' innocence, "Truly I tell you, today you will be with me in Paradise" (Luke 23:43).

While in physical agony and emotionally overwhelmed by feelings of betrayal, Jesus was also concerned for the troubled people responsible for his death. He begged God to forgive them: "Father, forgive them; for they do not know what they are doing" (Luke 23:34). Jesus did not use the words of forgiveness himself. Perhaps because he knew that, ultimately, forgiveness comes from God, perhaps because he was simply unable to use words of forgiveness, he asked God to forgive. The question remains unanswered: How angry was the dying Jesus?

In Matthew's passion story, Jesus is far more aware of his power. He says to those who arrest him that he could ask his Father for legions of angels (Matt. 26:53). He tells the high priest that he will be "seated at the right hand of Power and coming on the clouds of heaven" (Matt. 26:64; cf. Luke 22:69). And immediately after Jesus breathed his last, Matthew says the earth quaked and there was an instant resurrection of the saints (27:51–53).

Finally, in the Gospel ascribed to John, eight of the twenty-one chapters are given to the last Passover meal and the Passion and death of Jesus. At the beginning of the account, John has Jesus proclaim that when he is lifted up, he will draw all to himself (John 12:32). His death and resurrection are the ultimate sign of God's presence and purpose in his life. One finds less struggle and anger in John's account of the Passion, more theological discourse on the meaning of Jesus' life and the promise of the Spirit. Unique to John's Gospel, Jesus addresses his mother and the disciple John from the cross. He does not cry out in anguish but makes two further statements: "I am thirsty" and "It is finished."

And so end the Gospels. Jesus, born of Mary, sent by God to reveal what it is to be human, finished his work. His life and his death demonstrated what it meant to take God seriously, to be true to God and to God's vision without turning back.

My conviction remains that from infancy through his death, Jesus felt all of the emotions that human beings experience, anger among them. Beyond his earthly life, Christ, the risen One whose Spirit lives in the whole Christa community, continues to experience righteous anger at the disrespectful, destructive way in which human beings treat one another and the planet they have inherited. The Bible portrays a God who grows intensely angry and a Jesus who experiences the full range of human emotions. The next question is: What does the Bible teach about anger in ordinary human life?

6

Human Anger

A robust spirituality of anger faces a daunting future: overcoming our amnesia of irascible prophets and an angry Jesus; admitting conflict as a necessary dynamic in our religious life; disbelieving that violence can remedy our differences; recrafting civility as a political virtue; reinvigorating the ancient virtues of courage and temperance. Short of such a renaissance, we will be left with a moribund religious tradition of anger as a deadly sin and a cultural heritage of violence as the ordinary and acceptable voice of anger.

James D. Whitehead and Evelyn Eaton Whitehead
"Shadows of the Heart: A Spirituality of the Negative Emotions"

If anger is an intimate though mysterious part of the life of God, and if Jesus acknowledged and expressed anger in his ministry as God's spokesperson, then human beings can be both godlike and Christlike in acknowledging and expressing their anger. This chapter returns to the Bible in order to discern its messages about human anger.

Two approaches to the study of human anger in the Bible were employed here. The first approach was to study all references to the words *anger* and *wrath*. In the Hebrew Bible, the books of Proverbs and Psalms contain a majority of such passages. In the Christian scriptures, exhortations about anger appear primarily in the epistles.

Numerous biblical stories will be missed, however, if one looks only for the explicit use of the word *anger* or one of its synonyms. Angry people show up in many biblical narratives that do not include the word *anger*. A second approach was to read selected biblical stories, listening for the expression of anger or the failure to express anger that must certainly have been experienced by persons involved in the accounts.

What one quickly learns is that the Bible does not speak with a single voice on the topic of human anger. Earlier in the book I discussed two expressions of anger that emerge in infancy: the *anger of hope* and the *anger of despair*. Human anger in the Bible can be broadly divided into the same two expressions. Because the anger of despair appears in the opening book of the Bible, the following exploration begins at the beginning.

The Anger of Despair

Unless one reads Eve's refusal to obey God's injunction against eating the fruit as an angry act, the firstborn son of Adam and Eve is the first person in the Bible to express anger:

> In the course of time Cain brought to the Lord an offering of the fruit of the ground, and Abel for his part brought of the firstlings of his flock, their fat portions. And the Lord had regard for Abel and his offering, but for Cain and his offering he had no regard. So Cain was very angry, and his countenance fell. The Lord said to Cain, "Why are you angry, and why has your countenance fallen? If you do well, will you not be accepted? And if you do not do well, sin is lurking at the door; its desire is for you, but you must master it."
> Cain said to his brother Abel, "Let us go out to the field." And when they were in the field, Cain rose up against his brother Abel, and killed him.
>
> (Gen. 4:2–8)

The dominant message of the story is clear: the sins of the parents are transmitted from generation to generation. Rebellion against God leads to rebellion against one's sisters and brothers.

The story of Cain leaves me with nagging questions. Why did God have no regard for Cain's offering? Does disregard for an offering also convey rejection of its donor? Was the younger son given the favored task, the older assigned less-important work, that which was more readily assigned to women? Men tend to animals, women garden.

God's preferential treatment of Abel seems to follow the younger-son motif—the inverse of primogeniture, or the privileged place assigned to the firstborn. In Gen. 25:23, the Lord says to Rebecca that she will give birth to two sons from whom will come divided nations; "the one shall be stronger than the other, the elder shall serve the younger." God's plan gets worked out through a younger sibling. While such a reversal may be part of the message, nevertheless, if the Cain and Abel story is taken at face value, Cain is unfairly treated by God. God had no regard for Cain's offering.

At the same time that God rejected Cain's gift, God advised Cain to deal with his anger, namely, by working hard and seeking acceptance.

Cain did not address his anger at God. Instead, he displaced his anger, destroying Abel, the brother God favored.

Although the story is thoroughly male, the emphasis on acceptance makes it instructive for women as well. The point of the story seems to be that when one feels that God has favored another, that life is unfair, one must decide what to do with one's disappointment, one's sense of injustice, and the anger that comes with believing that one was not treated fairly. God's response to Cain says nothing about the rejection of Cain's offering; that seemingly arbitrary decision on God's part is not explained. Rather, God tells Cain that if he does well, he will be accepted. Cain's behavior determines whether it is well with him—not his offering.

When women recognize that the lack of regard they receive, easily experienced as rejection, is as arbitrary as the lack of regard that Cain experienced, they need to know what to do with their anger. Women's anger is often a response to perceived rejection, trivialization, or injustice. For reasons no clearer than those offered in the text, women's gifts are arbitrarily seen as second to men's gifts. Even their ideas are trivialized, simply because they come from women. Women repeatedly report making suggestions or sharing ideas in mixed-gender gatherings that meet with minimal response. A male colleague later makes the same suggestion a woman already offered, and his idea is affirmed, even praised. Once the idea has been proffered by a man, its value increases.

Cain's downfall was not his anger that God did not accept his offering. Cain failed himself, his brother, and his God because he did not use his anger well. He did not accept God's invitation to talk about his anger in order to understand it more fully. Instead, he was overwhelmed by it and acted out in murderous rage.[1]

Cain made a fatal choice. Rather than expressing the anger of hope through telling God about the hurt and resentment he felt when his offering was not accepted, he expressed the anger of despair, destroying the brother whose gift was favored by God. The danger in the story is that anger itself can be seen as the problem, as the sin lurking at the door. On the contrary, revenge was the sin lurking at the door. The anger was a deeply human response to the perception of unjust treatment.

The anger of despair was surely experienced by some of the women in the Bible who were raped, murdered, and sacrificed by their fathers, husbands, and brothers. The narratives themselves do not recognize or acknowledge the anger of the women, let alone allow them to express their feelings. The voice of the victims of abuse is totally silenced.

For example, the book of Judges tells the story of a Levite who took to himself a concubine from Bethlehem.[2] There was clearly no equality in this relationship. A Levite is above other males; a concubine, more slave than wife, is beneath other females.[3] The text does not say why the concubine became angry with her husband, only that she was angry and returned to her father's home. Four months later, her husband set out to woo her back. Apparently he knew that the relationship needed some serious attention.

The nameless concubine's father relished the company of his son-in-law. For four days and nights the men ate and drank together, apparently excluding the concubine from their companionship. Each time the visitor attempted to leave, his father-in-law encouraged him to spend more time with his host. There is no mention of the concubine or her wishes, or any indication that the Levite did "speak tenderly to her" (Judg. 19:3). In fact, she remains speechless and unspoken to throughout the story, a silent presence.

Finally, on his way home, the man, his concubine, and his servant were invited into an old man's home. When a gang of men from the city came to find the Levite to rape him, the old man gave the intruders his own virgin daughter and the concubine instead. The evil men refused the offer. The Levite stepped in and, in effect, saved himself at the expense of his concubine. Perhaps he saved the father's virgin daughter as well. The text tells us that he

> seized his concubine, and put her out to them. They wantonly raped her, and abused her all through the night until the morning. And as the dawn began to break, they let her go. As the morning appeared, the woman came and fell down at the door of the man's house where her master was, until it was light. (Judg. 19:25–26)

The conclusion of the story is as almost as horrifying as the rape. Without saying whether the concubine was dead or alive, the text tells the reader that her husband took her home, cut her body into twelve pieces, and scattered her body parts throughout Israel. He asked that his people speak out against what has happened; no hint of his own participation in the rape and murder of his concubine. In the next chapter, he condemned the men of Gibeah for their vile outrage but vindicated himself. Violence bred violence as thousands upon thousands were killed in one battle after another that were flamed by this tragedy.

One can surmise that when the concubine returned to her father's house, she left her husband in anger because she was abused or treated unjustly. That can only be surmised because the text gives her no voice. The anger she must have experienced as her father and husband enjoyed their days pales before the anger she knew when she was sacrificed to save her husband from a homosexual rape. Her voice was silenced forever. The anger of despair? Again, there is only silence. I turn now to the anger of hope.

The Anger of Hope

The Anger of Hope in the Hebrew Bible

While the story of the first offspring, Cain, belongs to the mythological narratives of creation, the prophet Jeremiah was a flesh-and-blood individual who lived from approximately 626 to 580 B.C.E. Jeremiah expresses the anger of hope. Consecrated before he was formed in his mother's womb, Jeremiah was trained by Yahweh to speak against all forms of injustice and evil. The prophet's words, interwoven with the "word of the Lord," come in wave after wave of warning, reminder, challenge—expressed in hope that the message will be heard and people will change their ways.

Both God's anger and Jeremiah's anger are clear expressions of the anger of hope, anger always in tension with passion for the people. God's anger will not last forever because God loves; Jeremiah's anger mingles with sorrow because Jeremiah cares.

While in Jeremiah 3, Yahweh promises that divine anger will come to an end, in the next chapter the people are told to proclaim that "the fierce anger of the Lord has not turned away from us" (Jer. 4:8). Jeremiah mourns, crying out to God in anger and sadness because of the behavior of the people the prophet is called to serve: "My joy is gone, grief is upon me, my heart is sick. . . . ('Why have they provoked me to anger with their images, with their foreign idols?') . . . For the hurt of my poor people I am hurt, I mourn, and dismay has taken hold of me" (Jer. 8:18–21).

Reading Jeremiah gives me a new understanding of cursing God. When people call out the name of God or Jesus in railing against injustice or evil, the cry may indeed be both a cry to God and a cry against God for what God has created. It is as if the cursing one is saying, "Oh God, how could you possibly allow such mean-spirited creatures to exist?" Just as the voice of Jeremiah blends with the voice of Yahweh, so may the voice of a cursing woman or man blend with the voice of God in angry cries against the hardness of heart that results in cruelty, greed, social injustice.

On the interpersonal level, the prophet's railing against perceived injustice finds its echo in the most profound intimate relationships between committed partners. In the heat of conflict, anger and sadness and love and hate swirl, often expressed by words that hurt—an expression of the anger of hope that the relationship not only will endure but will be changed.

Where is Jeremiah's anger of hope today? Professor Keith Russell asks, "Why is so little anger of the prophetic variety coming from contemporary pulpits?" Preachers are afraid of anger. Russell says, "I think preachers are afraid of anger to the point that by avoiding it as much as possible we cut ourselves off from anger's companions, passion and sorrow."[4]

Remember Carol Tavris's statement that emotions come in clusters, like grapes. Avoiding any one of them tends to result in avoidance of whole clusters of feeling. Preachers afraid of anger can become dulled to many intense feelings.

By contrast, the psalmist, unafraid of anger, brings deep feelings of bitterness and rage to God and makes the expression of emotion available to anyone who prays the psalms of lament. Nowhere in the Bible is the anger of hope more evident than in these angry cries of human pain and hurt and near despair. The laments are complaints addressed to God, a protest that what has happened is unfair and inexplicable.[5]

The major motivation behind writing this book was to discover ways for people to be honest and whole in their relationships to one another and before God, particularly when they are filled with what have been termed the negative emotions: anger, fear, hurt, despair. The lament psalms are a priceless gift to persons caught up in troubling emotion, precisely because they model raw, honest expression of feeling coupled with deep connection with and praise of God. It is connection with God and praise of God that make the rage of the laments an expression of the anger of hope rather than the anger of despair. Vengeful cries of punishment are coupled with a word of faith:

> Break the arm of the wicked and evildoers;
> . . . .
> O Lord, you will hear the desire of the meek.
> > (Ps. 10:15, 17)
> Let death come upon them;
> let them go down alive to Sheol;
> for evil is in their homes and in their hearts.
> . . . .
> But I will trust in you.
> > (Ps. 55:15, 23)

O God break the teeth in their mouths;
tear out the fangs of the young lions, O Lord!
· ·
Let them be like the snail that dissolves into slime;
like the untimely birth that never sees the sun.
· ·
"Surely there is a God who judges on earth."
                                        (Ps. 58:6–8, 11)

Let their table be a trap for them,
a snare for their allies.
Let their eyes be darkened so that they cannot see,
and make their loins tremble continually.
Pour out your indignation upon them,
and let your burning anger overtake them.
· ·
Let heaven and earth praise him,
the seas and everything that moves in them.
                                        (Ps. 69:22–24, 34)

If I forget you, O Jerusalem,
let my right hand wither!
· ·
O daughter Babylon, you devastator!
· ·
Happy shall they be who take your little ones
and dash them against the rock!
                                        (Ps. 137:5, 8, 9)

Contractual theology fills the psalmist's cries against evil: the wicked deserve the punishment called down on them because they have sinned against God and God's people.

The dynamic involved in these calls for retribution is puzzling. How does it help anyone to spew out venom and curses on their enemies before God, pleading that God be the vindicator? The help is fundamentally psychological. Call it human nature, the human condition, aggression. Some call it original sin. Deep feeling seeks expression.

Much of the pain expressed by the psalmist is conscious; reasons are offered for the anguished state. However, conscious anger easily taps into unconscious experiences of frustration and anger. The psalmist often speaks from the depths of human loss and grief, both conscious and unconscious.

The laments provide a place for angry people to release their rage freely in prayer, rather than in destructive deeds. While unable to reverse what has happened, through praying the laments, a person can do something about it. One can curse evil. I part with David Blumenthal in his suggestion that the imprecatory psalms are not verbal catharsis but acts of verbal vengeance. Distinguishing between performative speech and performative action, he says:

> A curse is performative speech, speaking is doing; it is not expressive language, verbal catharsis. To curse is to call down supernatural vengeance; it is not to vent one's deepest feelings. To curse is to call down violence on the oppressor, to invoke abuse on the abuser.
>
>   And yet a curse is not performative action; it is not accomplishing one's rage in social deed.[6]

In contrast, I would assert that the psalms of lament can be profoundly cathartic. They can indeed allow an expression of one's deepest feelings. They provide the opportunity for a person to let God know how deep the rage is, how vengeful the thoughts, how desperate the loss, how thin the hope.[7] The psalms are the most appropriate place in the Bible for those whose anger borders on despair to express their agony and find a glimmer of hope in God's presence and action.

I turn now to the anger of hope in the New Testament.

The Anger of Hope in the Gospel of Matthew

Jesus' most explicit words about anger appear only in Matthew's Gospel:

> You have heard that it was said to those of ancient times, "You shall not murder"; and "whoever murders shall be liable to judgment." But I say to you that if you are angry with a brother or sister, you will be liable to judgment; and if you insult a brother or sister, you will be liable to the council; and if you say, "You fool," you will be liable to the hell of fire. So when you are offering your gift at the altar, if you remember that your brother or sister has something against you, leave your gift there before the altar and go; first be reconciled to your brother or sister, and then come and offer your gift.
> (Matt. 5:21–24)

The tense of the verb *to be angry* used here implies that one is continuously angry or keeps on being angry.[8] Some manuscripts say "angry without cause," implying unfounded anger. Apparently, in this passage from Matthew's Gospel, Jesus is talking about people who live in long-term anger toward another that is not based in reality.

The danger of this understanding is that persons might use it to dismiss another person's anger as unfounded or not based in reality. For example, oppressed people live with long-term anger toward the systems that oppress them. Those who benefit from the system might say such anger is unfounded, that "that's just the way things are and have always been." People in power too easily can conclude that the powerless are angry without cause—surely a misreading of the gospel.

Jesus advises the angry person to seek reconciliation by dealing with whatever needs to be addressed in order to stop living in anger toward a sister or brother. One does not express the anger in abusive outbursts or get rid of it through denial. One expresses the anger of hope directly to the person or persons involved in a thoughtful way that allows reconciliation to happen. The judgment Jesus speaks of is based on the way one approaches a sister or brother, rather than on the fact that one expresses anger. The passage does not address legitimate anger following abusive behavior or anger at the abuse of power and unjust social structures.

Anger in the Epistles and in Church Teaching

What lesson has the church taught regarding the expression of anger? Once again, the answer is complex. A dominant message from the church has been that anger is a sin, a capital or deadly sin. From the medieval development of the seven deadly sins up to present time, anger has been located in the forbidden zone and treated primarily as sin.[9] Seldom do episcopal letters or other church documents encourage members of congregations to express their personal and social anger well. Seldom do preachers speak about the power of anger in Christian living.

Part of the confusion about anger stems from the ambiguous, even conflicting biblical messages on anger. In some cases the conflict is evident in a single text, as in the message in Ephesians:

> So then, putting away falsehood, let all of us speak the truth to our neighbors, for we are members of one another. Be angry but do not sin; do not let the sun go down on your anger. . . . Put away from you all bitterness and wrath and anger and wrangling and slander, together with all malice, and be kind to one another, tenderhearted, forgiving one another, as God in Christ has forgiven you. (Eph. 4:25–26, 31–32)

One must not lie but speak the truth. If part of that truth is anger, then denial of the feeling is a lie. Yet following fast upon the command to speak the truth is the instruction to put away anger. While the message might be that one is to deal with the anger rather than let it fester unaddressed, the summons is muted by the directive to get rid of the anger. One might question whether this is really a plea to speak the truth or whether the message is perhaps quite the opposite. Might it not be interpreted as a call to deny feeling or to use the words of forgiveness when the pain and grief suffered are not fully explored and expressed and worked through?

In the best of circumstances, the accomplishment of genuine friendship includes speaking the honest truth, whatever emotions are involved, directly to the person concerned. The passage from Ephesians, however, can be read as a minimalization of the experience of anger. Might this be Paul's rationale for avoiding his own anger (if indeed these are Paul's words)? What did he do with his anger at the church in Corinth, his anger at the apostles in Jerusalem, including Peter, for not accepting the inclusion of the Gentiles? How about his earlier anger at the Christians themselves, before his conversion? How did he deal with his anger toward John/Mark for deserting him on one of the journeys (Acts 15:37–39)? Did he simply forgive?

Forgiveness is a process that takes more time than the passage seems to suggest. Repressing one's anger simply in order to forgive an offense gives birth to bitterness and contaminates friendship. It also leaves the one who mouthed the words of forgiveness feeling guilty for not really doing what she or he claimed to do.

To avoid letting the sun set on her anger, a person often does one of two things: she gets rid of the anger somehow, through denial or suppression or if the anger was irrational, by changing her thinking; or she acknowledges that she was treated unjustly but chooses to surrender the anger rather than allow it to affect her emotional life. But there is a third, more hopeful alternative: she may choose to deal with the anger through honest communication. (A father advised his son to settle an issue as quickly as possible because the Bible says he should not let the sun go down on his anger. The boy responded: "But that's not fair. I can't stop the sun from going down.")

Combine the message of Ephesians with the words of Jesus according to Matthew: first, recognize the anger; second, direct it to its source; and third, seek reconciliation. There are the three steps; each of them can be filled with conflict and pain and can require difficult conversation, which many seek to avoid.

One way that the church teaches an ethics of anger is through the repeated use of a small number of biblical references, the passage from Ephesians at the top of the list. Another often-cited biblical reference is "One who is quick-tempered acts foolishly" (Prov. 14:17). A major form of the anger of hope advocated in both the Hebrew Bible and the New Testament is controlled anger, or as I call it, *slow-to anger*.

Surely everyone has been quick to anger and wished that she or he might take back hurtful words or deeds. How slow is slow? Does "slow to anger" mean pausing long enough to assess where the feelings are coming from and deciding what one wants to do in the moment? Or is "slow to anger" yet another patriarchal way of controlling anger?

There are biblical scholars, theologians, and church leaders who do not believe that human anger is an acceptable emotion. They base their conclusions largely on the Ephesians passage cited above and on the brief message from James: "Let everyone be quick to listen, slow to speak, slow to anger; for your anger does not produce God's righteousness" (James 1:19–20). Here is a sampling of opinions, all of them advocated by men:

Gustav Stählin, in *Kittel's Theological Dictionary,* says that "wrath is for God, but not for man (James 1:20). God's love includes wrath, but love and anger are mutually exclusive in man."[10]

Stephen Hinks, economics teacher in New South Wales, thinks that Paul's central message about anger is to get rid of it—"put it away from you." Hinks believes the biblical teaching is that anger harms human relationships. The best response to anger, then, is control, directed toward restraint.[11]

Writing for the same symposium as Hinks did, John Court, director of a counseling center in Adelaide, South Australia, disagrees. Court acknowledges that we far too readily react angrily to personal hurt; however, we respond to injustice too slowly. His conclusion is that "a healthy expression of anger without sin requires us to respond directly, openly and briefly." Whereas human anger too often intends to hurt or destroy, godly anger works toward change and resolution.[12]

The same debate has gone on among another theologians, with one claiming that

> people cannot be angry at personal offense apart from sin unless such anger arises where human will perfectly corresponds with divine will, unless human action perfectly corresponds with divine action and unless no human emotion accompanying this perfect will and action is contrary to the appropriate divine emotions under those circumstances. . . . Anger as a result of personal offense finds no justification in Scripture. Such offenses are to be accepted as part of the Christian's lot of suffering. Although we might express our displeasures at such actions, anger is inappropriate. The proper Christian response involves turning the offense and the offender over to God who alone can properly judge the offense and its underlying motives and provide a proper punishment.[13]

I quote this theological reflection in sufficient detail because such thinking needs to be put away, preferably before sundown. In the first place, who can possibly declare when human will or action perfectly corresponds to God's will or action? Such abstract theological and ethical thinking is damaging to women and men who are struggling to find their angry voices. It is death to women who have been sexually or physically abused; their anger can be their lifeline out of a hell of helplessness.

Over thirty years ago, feminist Valerie Saiving challenged the claim that pride is the foundational sin by pointing out that women's sin has long been self-rejection and trivialization, not pride.[14] Labeling anger a sin has created a parallel problem for women. Women have been discouraged from using their anger to assert themselves as proud, valuable people, equal to men in intellectual and emotional capacities as well as leadership abilities. Their sin is not anger but the denial of anger.

Generalizations are dangerous. It may be true that the sins which men in positions of power most struggle against are pride and anger: pride that makes it difficult for them to acknowledge their mistakes and humbly apologize, and even more difficult to accept women as their equals; anger that is too often expressed in a violent abuse of power. However, many factors are at play in cross-sex and same-sex relationships, factors that vary from culture to culture. I feel less cautious in generalizing that women have long needed a theology and a psychology that call them to full and equal partnership with men. They need to start with a recognition of their genuine worth and not by focusing on their potential evil.

To want women to use their anger in discovering their pride is not to idealize women. Women's self-respect and self-assertion do not have to come at the expense of acknowledging their own mixture of good and evil, of hurt and hope. The focus, however, is on possibility and the good use of personal and collective power to undo patriarchy and recreate institutions.

Hurt and hope, the mainsprings of the theology of the Hebrew Bible, are the mainsprings of human life. Beginning with the child's anger of hope and continuing right through to the adult's anger of hope that justice-love will prevail, anger can be holy energy. All women and men need to recognize, acknowledge, and use their anger well. They also need to hear the angry groan of the oppressed and to groan with them to bring about justice.

How does one know when the expression of anger is holy energy and when it is bitterness or hatred? Once one has established that an experience of anger is a godly call to action, how does one decide how best to act? Discernment and action are the dual themes of the final chapter.

Conclusion:
A Call to
Faithful Action

Anger expressed and translated into action in the service of our vision and our future is a liberating and strengthening act of clarification, for it is in the painful process of this translation that we identify who are our allies with whom we have grave differences, and who are our genuine enemies.

Anger is loaded with information and energy. . . . [One needs] to stand still, to listen to its rhythms, to learn within it, to move beyond the manner of presentation to the substance, to tap that anger as an important source of empowerment.

Audre Lorde
Sister Outsider

Back and forth I danced in shaping this final chapter. My goal is twofold: first, to offer practical steps that one might take in order to comprehend and discern the source and meaning of one's own anger; second, to present strategies for determining how to react or respond in situations when one wants to use the power of anger for the sake of just relations.

I toyed with adding a third goal, urged on me by women and men who find themselves near paralysis in the presence of angry people. They seek ways of maintaining a calm enough presence to an angry person that they neither deny nor avoid the anger. They also need workable ways to respond to an angry other, especially when the other is a partner or spouse.

Such conversations have only deepened my conviction that if persons can deal effectively with their own anger, they will overcome their fear or intimidation in the presence of angry persons unless the other is violent, in which case immediate outside help is needed. The problem that is typically presented to me is that of a person (most often a woman) who feels emotionally threatened in the presence of an angry partner (most often a man). Her fear is that if she responds honestly to his anger, she will have to express her own anger, and the relationship will be damaged or terminated. The difficulty goes back to a fear of her own anger.

A parallel quandary in handling angry persons stems from the fact that the person who expresses anger, fear, or any strong emotion often gains the high ground. The person receiving the expression of anger can feel manipulated or controlled by the display of anger. My hunch is that this is particularly true in cross-gender experiences of anger. Men sometimes fear a woman's anger because it forces them to be open and intimate, which is to be vulnerable. Once again, the problem goes back to the fear of expressing anger. When a person feels manipulated, believes that someone has taken the high ground in a controlling way, why not confront the other and express the anger aroused in the situation?

While what follows will surely relate to dealing with anger in another, the primary goal is to understand and use one's own anger well. *Understanding* and *doing* appear to be separate enough challenges to deserve separate chapters. The reality is that the process of discernment is, in fact, a doing; understanding and doing are distinguishable but connected steps in one interwoven process. Understanding and doing seemed to me to belong in the same chapter, indispensable parts of one model or process for dealing with anger.

This chapter addresses the ethical concern raised in the introduction of the book: How does one know whether a particular experience of anger is a good and holy urge to redress injustice and effect change, or whether an angry reaction to personal or social offense is narcissistic, a self-centered need to secure one's power or reputation? How does one discern the message that anger is speaking, or in Audre Lorde's language, how does one tap the load of information and energy that comes with anger?

Even after thoroughly considering the situation and reaching the conclusion that the expression of anger is not only appropriate but imperative, what strategies does a person use to effectively express her or his anger? In what way is the decision to express anger implemented?

In addition to knowing how best to deal with one's own anger, persons in caregiving relationships need ways best to respond to the anger of others. They must assess what is needed in specific situations and help persons with whom they counsel find ways to deal effectively with their anger.

A caveat is in order. This chapter is written for anyone seeking more effective ways of dealing with anger, both anger that arises in one's personal life and anger at the institutional or social-systems level. Persons whose anger is chronically out of control or who express their anger or rage destructively need immediate professional help. While some of the ideas presented here may be useful to them, the model will not be sufficient. Anyone who knows that his or her anger puts others at physical or psychological risk needs professional assessment and intervention. Anyone who has lost significant relationships because of an inability to control anger needs professional help in order to change destructive ways of expressing rage.[1] A return to definitions of holy anger and sinful anger is the necessary starting place.

The Continuum: From Holy Anger to Sinful Anger

In chapter 1, holy anger was defined as a response to the experience of being ignored, injured, trivialized, or rejected, as well as an empathic response aroused by witnessing someone else being ignored, injured, trivialized, or rejected. Anger is also a response to the awareness of social evils such as prejudice, oppression, and violence. Holy anger is a call to action.

Negative or sinful anger is a vengeful, hostile, sometimes explosive reaction to an interpersonal or social situation; it aims to injure persons or institutions and tears at the fabric of society by destroying relationships. Whereas holy anger seeks to right a wrong, whether the evil has been perpetrated on oneself or another, sinful anger is the expression of a wrongdoer, who inflicts evil on wronged people. Most often the wrongdoer is a brokenhearted person, herself or himself wronged.

While a distinction has been made between personal and social anger, sinful anger is always social in that relationships are involved. Brokenheartedness is the result of both complex, sinful social structures and specific sinful behavior on the part of individuals. Social structures, from family to school to church to the marketplace, frame human life and frame human anger. Early in childhood the brokenhearted person may not have been respected or loved sufficiently to live and behave humanly within mutually satisfying relationships. The effects of not having been wanted as a child, of having had an alcoholic parent(s), of undesirable circumstances surrounding one's birth, such as a lack of health care, poverty, violence—all these systemic conditions contribute to brokenheartedness. They also include choices on the part of some individuals that keep the brokenheartedness going from one generation to the next.

Everything said about anger includes systemic dimensions. Caught in a flawed family social system within a larger, deeply flawed social world, the brokenhearted adult was probably herself or himself disempowered rather than nurtured as a child and may bring a child into that same brokenness. The brokenhearted child-become-adult lashes out in anger that further damages the social systems which frame and undergird her or his life.

Perhaps the sinner rarely understands the depth of his or her wrongdoing. Damaged by harmful relationships, the destructively angry person demonstrates in true systemic fashion that the sins of one generation are visited on the next. How hard it is to get back to the roots of destructive anger that has spread through the generations!

Anger that manipulates moves toward sinful anger. I say "moves toward" because manipulation happens with great frequency in many human interactions. People set out to get other people to behave in certain ways. I manipulate the students in my class from the moment I hand out the syllabus up to the self- and course-review session that concludes the semester. From gentle persuasion to gross coercion, human beings manipulate others in order to shape events according to one or another design. To assess the quality of the manipulation, discernment is required.

Anger that results from misunderstanding or from the projection of repressed resentment, hurt, or rage falls somewhere along the continuum between holy anger and deadly sin. One needs to look at anger contextually and systemically to understand what is being expressed, what need or value is behind the behavior of both the perceived wrongdoer and the injured person, what kind of power an angry person feels when others are affected by his or her anger. Once again, there is a need for discernment. (Obviously, discernment can take place only when the anger is recognized in the first place. For many women especially, the anger is named only in retrospect.)

Self-awareness, particularly with regard to one's aggression and anger, coupled with respect for the other are what primarily account for the difference between healthy and sinful anger: in one case, a careful, assertive confrontation for the sake of justice and honest relationship; in the other, a hostile, sometimes hateful attack on a person or institution perceived as the enemy. Yet in most cases there is a mixture of justice seeking and self-seeking—and hence the need for discernment. What follows is an understanding-and-doing model for working through anger.

A Model for Dealing with Anger

On many occasions people know intuitively and spontaneously that they are angry, why they are angry, and what they want to do or not to do with their anger. That sounds like "no problem," and in some cases there is no notable problem. Communication is direct and straightforward, anger is expressed and heard, and life goes on.

Anger, however, is often far more complicated. The context can (be allowed to) dictate either the denial or the suppression of anger. Within all relationships—intimate, casual, or work-focused—spoken and unspoken ground rules determine how one deals with anger, in response to a friend, family member, or colleague. For example, a client once told me that at his law firm, dealing with interpersonal, emotional issues was clearly out of the question. An unwritten, unspoken law seemed to prevail. Along with his colleagues, he believed it was inappropriate to confront a work partner about personal matters. Conflicts festered, but conversations remained rational and guarded. On many occasions he knew that he was angry and why he was angry, and he knew that he would keep his anger to himself.

On perhaps as many occasions, persons know that they are angry, have a sense of why they are angry, but do not know what to do with their anger. If they are uncomfortable with their own anger, then they will surely be uncomfortable with the anger of others. The following proposal includes three essential steps in understanding and using anger well:

1. Hear the call: spend time with your experience of anger in order to understand yourself and the situation at hand.
2. Discern God's lure: determine whether this is a call to action or a call to surrender.
3. Strategize your response: plan, act, evaluate; if you choose to surrender your anger, then determine whether you need to do anything further to bring closure to the experience.[2]

Numerous possibilities for coming to understand one's anger are included here. The severity of the situation will determine which one or more of these options might be helpful on any particular occasion when one is angry. Granted, there is often insufficient time to work through many of the possibilities offered. If some of the suggestions are applied some of the time, then one will learn new ways of owning and expressing anger with creativity and satisfaction. The options might be seen as the spread at a Sunday brunch.

This model would not be appropriate if a person is threatening to injure herself or himself or others in destructive rage. In that case, the person needs immediate restraint and professional crisis care.

Hear the Call

Spend time with your experience of anger. This is a time of retreat, an intentional withdrawal from other activities for the sake of focused, personal reflection—a time to be silent, to feel, to think, to pray, to sort out the cluster of feelings that has emerged, the melange of thoughts that has cropped up, the deep-felt needs to which this experience points.

Begin by hearing your body. Because anger is always a physiological experience, your body is already involved by the time you know you are angry. Pay attention to the information it offers when anger flares. Note the changes in breathing, in heartbeat, in muscle tension, in the tightness of the jaw; feel the adrenaline rush. For some, there may be flatness and depression or listlessness; for others, intense agitation, anxiety, even excitement. The point is to own the anger alive in your body by attending to it. Your body has sounded an alarm. Something significant is at stake.

As you claim your bodily experience, feeling the sensations in all of their intensity, you can begin a calming process. Simply attend to your breathing, taking deep breaths that you hold for several seconds before exhaling. Come quietly home to yourself, breathing deeply to relax your tense body.

Perhaps most important is the desire to learn from your experience and the willingness to be open to either confronting and using your anger or to surrendering (but not repressing) it. Which way you go depends on the insight you gain through the discerning you do in this process.

Come home to yourself and to God's Spirit, who has made a home in you. A faithful and promising way to deepen your retreat is in open, honest prayer. You might pray one of the psalms of lament, where the psalmist curses evil and evildoers in a cry for justice and relief:

O Lord, God of my salvation,
when, at night, I cry out in your presence,
let my prayer come before you;
incline your ear to my cry.

> For my soul is full of troubles,
> and my life draws near to Sheol.   (Ps. 88:1–3)

In the midst of betrayal, one might pray:

> Do not be silent, O God of my praise.
> For the wicked and deceitful mouths are opened against me,
> speaking against me with lying tongues.
> They beset me with words of hate,
> and attack me without cause.   (Ps. 109: 1–3)

There are occasions when praying the psalms can be the most re-sourceful way of dealing with anger, a balm in the midst of desperation. Hebrew Scripture scholar Denise Dombkowski Hopkins writes:

> When my brother died, I was very angry at God. Without the psalm laments, I doubt that I could have remained in the church and continued to teach in seminary. The laments kept me talking to God, even if all my talk was angry talk. There was comfort for me in knowing that I was not alone in my anger and my doubt, that the saints before me had prayed these psalms.[3]

The psalms of lament can be prayed and then rewritten to match your present experience. What cry do you make to the Holy One, given your current experience?

A seminary student explains how the psalms helped her healing process. As a child she was sexually abused by a neighbor whom she turned to as a comforting authority figure after the death of her father. While the relationship began well, the man soon sexualized a trusting friendship into an abusive, secretive relationship that was torturous to the child. In adulthood she worked through the trauma therapeutically and continues her recovery, following paths that she finds through her deep faith in God. One avenue has been the lament psalms.

Psalm 77 has been particularly helpful. Rewriting the psalm helped her understand both its spontaneous and its deeper appeal. As with the psalmist, remembering former, better times with God helped her through agonizing nights. She too reached the point where she was able to "sing God's praise and be filled with the warmth of God's presence." However, the psalm did more:

> I shared with the psalmist the frustration of not knowing what to say to an-other survivor of sexual abuse—or to me—about where God was and is and what kind of God we worship. Where are the wonders being worked? Not with us! Or, are they? Is God a great and mighty god? In nature I see the power of God, as the psalmist, and sometimes am inspired to see God's hid-den footsteps working in my life.

Psalm 77 Revisited for Survivors

Carol B. Wilson[4]

I cry aloud to God,
Aloud to God that God may hear me.
Is God sleeping? Deaf?
I am hurting so in my very being.

Constantly I search for God.
In the day of my trouble I seek the Lord;
In the night my hand is stretched out without wearying;
My very being refuses to be comforted.

I remember God, and I cry aloud.
Nothing. No response.
I panic and my spirit barely resists death.

Are you, God, keeping my eyelids from closing?
I am so troubled and confused that I cannot speak or think.
I value the days of old,
I will remember our years of long ago.

I remember my music in the night.
But, now. Now, there is only fear in the night.
I panic and my spirit desperately searches for your strength.

Will the Lord spurn forever,
And never again be favorable?
Has God's covenant love ceased forever?
Are God's promises at an end for all time?
Has God forgotten to be gracious?
Has God in anger shut up his compassion?
But I say, "My grief is this:
The strength of the Most High God is changing."

No, that cannot be! I cannot stand the thought.
I will remember the deeds of the Lord;
I will remember your wonders of old.
I will meditate on all your work,
And muse on your mighty deeds.

As I remember, you will have to come to me.
Your way, O God, is holy.
Who is a great god like God?
You are the God who is working wonders;
You displayed your might among the people,
With your strong arm you pulled your people to you,
The survivors of unspeakable horrors.

Your reputation, O God, is suffering.
The skeptics surround us and are not afraid.

We do not know where to turn. Our lives are chaos.
Create peace within us, survivors.

When the waters saw you, O God,
When the waters saw you, they were afraid;
The primal waters of chaos did tremble.
The clouds poured out water;
The skies thundered; your arrows flashed everywhere.
The crash of your thunder was in the whirlwind;
Your lightnings lit up;
The world trembled; the earth shook.
Your way was through the sea,
Your path through the mighty waters;
Yet your footprints were unseen.

Where are you, O mighty Creator?
You led your people in the past.
You kept them from getting into trouble and danger.
You gave them protectors and helpers.
Lead us now! Protect our children.

Caregivers can facilitate the expression of anger at God for persons who do not feel free to speak to the Holy One in anger or rage.[5] As one counselor reports:

> I have found that when clients see my empathy with their anger at God, they begin also to feel God's compassionate understanding of their anger at [God]. Having permission to be angry at God allows clients to go beyond repressing, internalizing, or intellectualizing their anger to actually experiencing their anger and exploring its causes and consequences. [6]

Central to the successful understanding of what is going on inside as well as outside is the willingness to be totally honest with oneself. This involves a recognition of need, of searing pain, of the sense of betrayal, perhaps of brokenheartedness or even wrongheadedness in the interpretation one projects onto the experience of anger.

Having opened oneself before God with a deep desire to understand better the significance of the event(s) under consideration, your task is to seek clarity about what is going on with you. The following questions explore your feelings and thoughts about what has transpired.

1. How badly do you hurt? You may try describing your pain in detail. Some people find it useful to use fantasy in exploring pain.[7] As one writer suggests:

> Ask yourself, how deep is the pain? Is it on the surface, or below the skin? What shape does it have? What color is it? Use your imagination and guess a color, even if you do not see one. How large is it? Feel the tension totally.

Focus on the tension without analyzing it. Let the tension tell you what it is about. Become aware of any images or memories that arise while you continue to focus. You may find it helpful to breathe into that spot.[8]

2. On a scale of one to ten, how significant is this experience? The point of this question is not to minimize the event but to see it in a larger perspective and determine how much effort in working through the experience warrants.

3. Does the anger make good enough sense? That is, given this brief distance from the precipitating event, do you continue to believe that you have sufficient cause to be angry? Is your anger in proportion to the event that provoked it? If not, then can you discover what else is going on with you?

4. What value has been challenged, threatened, or destroyed in this experience? What change needs to be effected for the situation to be just and acceptable?

5. Does this experience feel like something from the past? This is an important question that is not always easily answered. How much of the threat that you feel now stems from losses in the past? How much belongs in the present?

6. Who is the enemy? Christians are taught to love their enemies and be good to those who hate them. To say that one has no enemies may sound as if one is close to perfection. To me it sounds wrongheaded. Enemies are all around. Granted, there are greater and lesser enemies, from indifferent, uncaring persons who do not wish one well to archenemies who seek to injure or destroy. The enemy need not be the person perpetrating what you perceive as evil but may be the injustice or dishonesty you perceive in a person's behavior.

An enemy is a person or institution that blocks others from realizing their potential or meeting their goals. Persons who disregard the needs of the homeless are enemies of the homeless. Racists are enemies of persons who are not of their own race. Sexists are enemies of women seeking liberation from patriarchy. Women, too, can be sexist. Can you name the enemy? Again, you need to assess whether the enemy is a person or institution in your current life, or whether the enemy is a person who disappointed or offended you in the past.

7. How much are your ego needs caught up in your emotional reaction? Can you be objective in analyzing what has happened? These questions may need to be explored in conversation with a trusted friend.

8. Is forgiveness appropriate? Is reconciliation indicated? Both premature offers of forgiveness and acceptance of forgiveness complicate the

resolution of anger. Unfortunately, well-meaning Christians pressure people into using forgiveness language long before they are ready, long before they really mean what the words convey.

Pastoral theologian John Patton's book *Is Human Forgiveness Possible?* suggests what is required for the offer of forgiveness to be genuine. Most important is that the person who is hurting express to a partner the depth and breadth of the pain that followed the offense. Pastoral counselors can facilitate the process, helping couples arrive at a place where the grace of forgiveness has been efficacious, whether or not the words of forgiveness have been spoken. "To tell persons to forgive is to proclaim salvation by good works. To help them discover that they have forgiven is to acquaint or reacquaint them with a power already operating in their lives."[9] Only after a person has been able to name the disappointment, the shame, the rage, the sense of betrayal, and to know that the message has been received is reconciliation won.

Responding to the above questions may yield the understanding needed. You may be ready to express your anger or to surrender it. However, you may want to do further exploration, using one or more of the following suggestions. Some of these possibilities are more active, others more receptive; all of them aim at deeper self-understanding. Choose what feels right to you. The options are primarily for individuals seeking ways to deal with personal anger; however, they could also be used by a person whose anger is primarily targeted at unjust social structures.

Option 1.
Move: Engage in Bodily Exercise

Physical activity creates a pause or break in the anger buildup. You might take your anger for a brisk walk and let the inner conversation, already underway, run its course; or if not a walk, then a run, a swim, a skate, a bike ride, a dance—any preferred exercise. Movement could mean spending time on a hobby or doing something as simple as bouncing a ball.

If anger flares at a time or place where movement or other activity is not feasible, then you might try isometric exercises that can be done at a desk, on a plane, almost anywhere. Tightening and relaxing the muscles in the body, muscle group by muscle group, can result in deep centering and relaxation. In whatever physical response you choose to make, pay attention to the message your body is speaking.

Option 2.
Audiotape a Conversation with Yourself

Pull out all the stops and tape-record a conversation with yourself about what happened. What you are thinking and feeling? When you have felt this way before? What experiences from the past throw light on what is happening now? Include anything you can say about your current and past experience. Brainstorm with yourself about what is going on. Let the tape run for at least fifteen but no more than thirty minutes, without being anxious about long pauses. Then listen to your tape four times:

> First, listen for the pain beneath the anger. Jot down what you heard.
> Second, listen for the interpretations or claims about life and rela-
>   tionships that are involved in your assessment of the situation.
>   (For a further explanation of interpretations, see Option 4 below.)
> Third, listen for the value(s) you hold that has been threatened by this
>   experience.
> Finally, listen for the sense of self that undergirds your speaking.[10]

Reflect on this experience and write a statement summarizing your learning.

The "listening four times" exercise might be even more useful if you ask someone who knows you well to listen to the tape at least once and attend to the same four issues. You could then compare your summary with that person's thoughts. This would provide the basis for the talk option outlined at Option 7, below.

Option 3.
Cluster and Write

Rewriting a psalm of lament was suggested earlier in this chapter as a way of working through anger. There are numerous possibilities for those with an interest in writing their way through anger. Some might write a story or fable. Two additional writing possibilities are included below in Options 5 and 6. (Others may respond more to color or image than to words and might try expressing their anger in artistic design.)

Another excellent way to focus your thoughts and feelings is by immersing yourself in what Gabriele Rico calls a clustering exercise.[11] The purpose of clustering is to engage the more imaginative, artistic, creative part of your mind (right-brain function) before trying to express yourself in a clear, rational way (left-brain function).

A clustering exercise begins when you write any word or phrase at the center of a blank piece of paper and circle it. In this case, simply write the word *anger* and circle it. Then let whatever spills out fill the page, circling words that spin off from or describe your anger. Lines with arrows connect the circled words. You may find yourself jotting words that have some connection when suddenly a seemingly new chain of thought emerges—both clusters of words going back to anger. Let as many branches spin off from anger as come up in your imagination. (See figure 1 on following page.)

Rico believes that clustering evokes a fresh, childlike attitude of wonder out of which many connections are made. As you continue to cluster, you will discover a pattern or insight that will be felt as an "aha," a moment of recognition that brings you closer to yourself within your experience of anger. The "aha" is a moment of transition. While the right brain spills images onto paper, the left brain inserts itself into the experience, with an illumination or insight marking a transition from random to logical thinking. A web of words without seeming connection suddenly illuminates what is happening. In figure 1, the "aha" came when the words *hold me* were written amid the web of words that spilled out around the word *anger*.

With the recognition, which is always accompanied by feeling, you move from a sense of haphazardness to a sense of direction, of wholeness. You then put your trial web vision into two or three focusing statements—in the illustration, "Hold me when I'm angry. Hush, hush the words."

Sometimes the writing that follows the trial web shift comes out in prose, sometimes in poetry. In either case you see your anger in a new way. The exercise may take you further: the anger web may give way to other webs, with a name or experience being circled at the center of yet another page. For example, after working with the word *anger*, a person may need to put a significant name or symbol or phrase from the past on a new page to seek further insight.

In this illustration, after clustering, I wrote:

Hold me when I'm angry.
Hush, hush the words,
Help me pause and know how deep the pain, the fear, the desperation.
Help me.
Just be there—solid arms and beating heart.
Help me talk through, or weep through, or laugh,
And in the laughter know that I can choose my true self: angry, aggrieved, at peace, a happy womanchild nurtured in this love-hold.
Hold me.

The words followed clustering at a time when I was not caught in the rush of anger; in fact, I was facilitating a workshop for clergywomen on anger,

Hold me when I'm angry.
Hush, hush the words

Fig. 1: Clustering exercise completed.

which was going well and increasing my energy and enthusiasm for the writing of this book. I did the exercise along with the participants.

On another occasion, however, angry feelings swirled like a brewing storm when my husband left for what felt like one too many evening meetings. I clustered. This statement followed the moment of illumination:

> Control again. Old familiar friend. The powerless teenager wanting parents to stay home—together.
>
> When Frank goes out after a meal that took much longer to prepare than to scarf down—and put together after my busy day that I intentionally end before he seems able to end his busy day—I'm thrown back, blistering.
>
> A teenager wanting a family to want to be together. (Where is my father, really? What is really behind my mother's depression?)
>
> She coped by playing cards at night. If she went out to play, then I felt deprived, alone (though not really—some sister or brother was almost always around) in a large, threatened home. If she played at home, then at least I got to serve her friends a snack at nine o'clock. Their presence somehow made the house feel more alive, more family.
>
> I wanted something else from her. I wanted something else from him. I wanted something else for all of us.
>
> Tonight my challenge is to let it go, change my expectations, know that the teenager thrived. I want Frank to understand and to be freely Frank—generous, committed to God, to me, to us, to justice-love.

What the clustering exercise does is help unpack the complicated experience of anger. One can then differentiate the bodily feelings, the beliefs or interpretations that contribute to the feelings, the needs the experience of anger reflects. The next suggestion is a follow-up to clustering the word *anger:* that is, to look at the interpretations that power the anger.

Option 4.
Get to the Beliefs That Relate to This Experience of Anger

Rational-emotive therapy recommends very specific ways of challenging the beliefs that are associated with feelings of anger.[12] If I believe that my partner will not go out often to evening meetings when I am left alone (and especially, not leave before the food is put away and dishes done), then I will be angry when this occurs with any frequency. I need to get behind the belief, however, which is what clustering helps me do.

When the anger flared on the occasion described above, I had no idea that my parents' difficult marriage and its effect, our often anxious family life, were behind the sudden anger. Much of early family life was covered years ago in what I continue to believe was quite effective therapy. And yet, an unrecognized aspect of the past lived on. What I saw and felt in a new way on a specific night alone in 1993 was that irrational beliefs most often go back into the early years of life and continue to keep us frustrated and angry unless the beliefs are revised.

When you are caught by your anger and have worked through the clustering and whatever writing followed the "aha," your next step is to list the various beliefs that relate to this experience of anger. Then go over the list and assess which of these beliefs are irrational and which reflect values you do indeed hold; in my case.

1. My husband will not spend many evenings away when I am at home. *Irrational*. He is very active in church, where most meetings are held in the evening.
2. After a long work day, I want to relax with my partner at night. *Rational*. The rhythm I seek in our life together is healthy and reasonable.
3. Work should be over after dinner. *Irrational*. On many occasions I make use of evening hours to complete work on something urgent or simply engaging.
4. People who work morning and afternoon ought not to work at night. *Rational*. Somewhere in my past I heard that eight-eight-eight is the healthy formula: eight hours of sleep; eight hours of work; and eight hours for an assortment of other things, including relating to partners and children; shopping for, preparing, and enjoying meals; and engaging in relaxing pursuits. For a working woman with children at home, the third eight hours seem to disappear.

Now I have a solid basis for a conversation about mutual expectations for evenings. Even more important, I understand my anger around this particular issue and can deal with evening meetings with new energy and peace of heart, though not without some continuing struggle.

On the societal level, suppose the anger is based on the unavailability of affordable child care for working parents. The beliefs behind their anger might run something like this:

1. Society shares responsibility for the basic welfare needs of its members. *Rational*. On a secular level, foundational to any society is responsibility for the fundamental needs of its members. On a faith level, belief in the body of Christ compels Christians to recognize their relationship within God's family with all of their sister and brothers.

2. The federal government, in cooperation with state and local agencies, should provide for child care needs of taxpaying, working parents at reasonable costs. *Rational.* Almost all industrial countries provide this benefit.

3. Based on the volume of their profits, for-profit businesses ought to subsidize child care costs. *Rational.* Most families need two incomes. Parents working for corporations could reasonably expect child care benefits as part of their employment package. (I find it difficult to come up with an irrational belief that would flame the anger of any reasonable person about the need for subsidized child care.)

Once beliefs have been examined, irrational ones can be revised and rational beliefs used in support of your efforts to effect change.

Option 5.
Dialogue with Your Anger

Another helpful way of understanding anger is to use the Ira Progoff method of dialogue. In *At a Journal Workshop,* Progoff provides a self-help technique for journaling out of a Jungian framework.[13] The book is intended for use over a one-and-one-half-day workshop. Each participant spends time alone in written dialogue between the self and some aspect of her or his inner life, between conscious and unconscious life, between the peaks and valleys of life. Parents, alive or dead, can be helpful dialogue partners. One can dialogue with events, with institutions, with any partner who has become an internalized other.

The Progoff dialogue is not recommended for use by persons who have not undertaken the workshop or worked through the whole process outlined in his book. But I have found the method to be far more flexible than that. Those familiar with Progoff might choose to dialogue with their anger. A dialogue with anger, which is in effect a dialogue with oneself, allows an angry person to be more objective, even humorous; to see new possibilities; to solve problems; to take back control over one's behavior and one's life.

Beth, a middle-aged European-American woman, spoke with me after she completed a summer internship. She was extremely angry when she received what she considered (and continues to consider) an unwarranted and irrational evaluation from one of her peers. Her colleague mailed the evaluation to Beth after the group had disbanded, leaving her with few options for dealing with her anger. Beth decided to dialogue

with her anger as an attempt to better understand herself. Then she might
be prepared to pick up her unfinished business with her colleague.

BETH: How is it between us, Anger?

ANGER: You've always had problems with me. I've been your companion
through your entire life, but I don't feel good about the relationship
because you are so uneasy about me. And you don't really understand
how to use me in a healthy and productive way. Yet I'm one of the
gifts God has given you.

BETH: You have been something I've had to contend with all my life. Dad
had temper tantrums from who-knows-what age. He brought them
into the marriage, having the first, according to my mother, six
months after they were married. These were almost always directed
toward my mother and usually happened at mealtime. I sat there,
witnessing his tantrums, watching his visible anger toward my
mother, watching him toss things, sometimes break them, in the
kitchen.

I seemed unable to move from my chair—riveted in my seat as
this awful scene was played out in front of me. It felt scary, it felt
awful, and I would be shaking inside. I was caught up in the moment,
the wave of emotion pouring out of my father. It shook me for an
hour or so after. He was no role model for handling anger.

ANGER: But what did you learn about anger from your mother? Wasn't
that quite a different approach?

BETH: It was! She seemed so controlled. She could get angry, and her eyes
flashed. To me, she was "too good" in her ability to handle anger—a
model I couldn't approach.

She said she disciplined my temper out of me—that I had quite a
temper as a child and she "rid" me of it. I suppose she'd seen such a
negative side of anger that she couldn't bear the thought of one of her
children being like their father. . . .

ANGER: I'm a basic part of human emotion. I'm necessary for fight and
flight for survival. When people don't have good models for handling
everyday anger or when they dislike themselves, the anger may come
out in distorted ways. Did your dad dislike himself?

BETH: My dad had very low self-esteem. It rubbed off on me. What a lack
of self-confidence! Especially beginning in the teen years.

I feel there's a relationship among my fears—the fear that dominated me so long through panic attacks, and my struggle with my
own and Dad's anger. The fear of being out of control.

ANGER: If I am suppressed, and you feel unable to express me, I don't go away. You'll just experience me in other forms—depression, panic attacks, fear of loss of control. I am powerful and give you power if you will use me to enable you to express yourself authentically. Given your background, that's not an easy task and never has been for you—except perhaps in your preschool years before your mother "rid" you of your anger/temper.

Was there anything positive that came out of the panic attacks?

BETH: The only thing I can say is that they gave me an empathy for the mentally ill. I know what it was like to deal with a "demon," to feel possessed, even though my possession didn't show as much to others—not like the Geresene demoniac. The hurt was directed mostly inward. I seemed to be punishing myself.

But I need to talk to you about my relationship to Steve [former husband]. You played a big role in that as well.

ANGER: Yes, he too had his difficulties with me. Coming from Irish stock with an alcoholic father and an ever-suffering but patient and dear mother, he also tried to "be in control" as an adult, expressing anger in a very rational manner. It spilled into his body language and you knew he was angry—and he was angry a lot.

BETH: He was very angry at me. I made a lot of mistakes where he's concerned. I'm the first to admit it. I hurt him, mostly without meaning to. And I tried to be in control—I tried to do too much. I always overscheduled myself, and then I'd feel a need for help. I was angry at being overwhelmed and I didn't like myself, I didn't seem to do a good job at anything, and most of all, I think I was a poor mother. The issue for me, again, was anger. . . .

Beginning in the late seventies, Steve began to be rather constantly angry at me. I felt this keenly, and I didn't know how to deal with it except to seek a more loving and peaceful relationship elsewhere.

ANGER: Being angry at children is not surprising. They do many things to frustrate you. . . .

Setting limits for you was never easy—just as it wasn't for your father! Your mother dominated him. The only way he felt he could get her attention or regain control was through his tantrums. That's the way he asserted himself. Otherwise he was very passive.

You, too, were very passive with your children. You'd let them get by with all kinds of things, not setting limits, feeling uncomfortable about doing so, and then some little incident would make you "blow."

Your anger at Steve was probably mixed up in this. You felt you couldn't get really angry at him and did so only when the pressure became so great, you became hysterical. Some of the anger toward Steve and the hurt you felt from his lack of attention, his seeming uncaring, and his relationships with other women probably spilled out toward your kids.

BETH: I suppose. And sometimes it would spill out toward others—when I'd feel overwhelmed. . . . But as my children aged, my job absorbed me and I had wonderful things happening in my life—a growing spiritual journey, opportunities to travel around the world, and a loving relationship. The panic attacks lessened and my passive-aggressive behavior lessened but didn't disappear. . . .

Even this summer in my internship, my continuing struggle with you was clear. I found myself angry at my supervisor but not expressing myself in a way that was effective. I thought I was debating him, standing up for my rights; he thought I sounded shrill.

Then I had an ongoing conflict with one of the members of my peer group. I got disgusted with her narcissism and domination of our group. But I could not seem to achieve a calm presence in relaying my anger.

ANGER: I think there are people who know how to use me in a way that sounds more rational, but nearly all people have their limits—especially when they're stressed out, exhausted, or physically ill.

I hope you'll try to consider how I've been a positive influence in your life. You've achieved much, and I think I can take some credit for that. Also, you're a person of passion, and that has some relationship to me.

You need to continue to learn about how I can help you. But you will live with me to your dying days, of that you can be certain. Learn to accept me!

While Beth's conflicted relationship with the woman in her peer group is still an unresolved issue, she reports that the dialogue has helped her look at her anger in a new way. Beth thinks she can be more patient with herself and has a clearer sense of what she needs to do. Perhaps one of her next steps is to go through a Progoff dialogue with her colleague, bringing Beth one step closer to a one-on-one conversation.

For those who use the Progoff method with some consistency, keeping a journal of dialogues becomes a way of life. The next option suggests yet another possibility for writing your way through anger.

Option 6.
Begin an Anger Diary

People who like to keep journals will have any number of ways of keeping diaries in which they record their experiences of anger. The most important aspect of journaling would be follow-up conversations with a professional or a trusted friend who could help the writer sort through the experiences recorded and arrive at insight.

I recommend a specific possibility. While this exercise involves individual work, it might best be done within a group. A small number of people (no more than eight recommended) agree to be alone a half hour each day for two weeks, at approximately the same time each day, when each would write about her or his anger, using the following guidelines.[14]

Note one time during the past twenty-four hours when you were aware of anger. Describe the event in one short paragraph, then answer the following questions:

1. On a scale of one to ten, how intense was the feeling?
2. What did you do with your feelings?
3. Were you satisfied with your behavior?
4. Would you consider this a holy experience, a sinful experience, or something in between?

The group would meet three times: at the beginning, middle, and end of the two-week period. Each member would share at the final group meeting a written reflection on what she or he had learned. A follow-up meeting approximately one month later would help group members evaluate their work and make adjustments in their plans as needed.[15]

Option 7.
Talk: Share Your Thoughts with a Trusted Friend

Speak about this experience of anger with a friend with whom you enjoy mutual honesty. You are not seeking advice so much as a caring presence, a sounding board, an honest response from another perspective. You seek what is called *reflective listening*. Your listener reflects back to you what she or he hears you say, as well as what the listener perceives to be the message beneath the message. It is most helpful when the listener responds initially by summarizing the heart of what you are saying, your central thoughts and feelings, thereby helping you see yourself more clearly in this incident.

Speak of the increased understanding about your anger that you have discovered. Talk through what you think you most want to do with your anger. What do you see as viable options? Review the options one at a time and pay attention to your inner responses. Again, your listener is simply moving with you through these options, helping you turn unturned stones as you assess what you want to do.

Proponents of this method of intentional, nonjudgmental listening claim that "there is nothing that defuses acute anger more effectively than reflective listening."[16] If you chose to keep an anger diary within the context of a small group, then your conversation partners may come through the group rather than in a one-on-one conversation.

It is generally in conversation that discernment takes place. Talking becomes a discerning. Yet discerning is listed here as a separate, second step in the model for understanding and using anger well, lest intentional discernment get lost in the process. Discernment questions help a person arrive at what she or he considers the most faithful response in a given situation.

The next task, then, is to put the work you have done to the discernment test, which helps you both arrive at a decision and determine where on the continuum between holy and sinful anger a given experience is located.

Discern God's Lure

Where is God leading you?

I hesitate to use the name Ignatius of Loyola in proposing a process of discernment because to be true to Ignatius's method, one would consider the intricate and elaborate structure, stage by stage, that constitutes his *Spiritual Exercises*.[17] That is not my intent. Ignatius, founder of the Society of Jesus, designed rules for discernment to be used once in a lifetime, when a person makes a life-orienting, vocational decision, namely, priesthood or marriage. Ignatius recommended an annual retreat based on the *Exercises* as a way to support the life decision already made.

As a person who for nineteen years made annual retreats based on the *Spiritual Exercises* (one of them a twenty-eight-day retreat that followed Ignatius's four-week spiritual program), I have appropriated some of the directives of the *Spiritual Exercises* as a way of life. Ignatius's steps in making significant decisions are particularly useful in discerning the path of anger in life. Persons who teach the Ignatian rules may consider them far removed from decisions about the expression or surrender of anger. I have found them to be useful springboards.[18]

My translation or appropriation of these ways of making a choice is as follows:

1. Bring into your imagination the situation with which you are concerned. This might involve reliving through memory the events that resulted in anger, while staying aware that God is intimately present to the situation.
2. Recognize your highest aim: the fullness of life in God's presence. At the same time, seek an open and unbiased state of mind, ready to follow what you discern to be a godlike response to the situation at hand.
3. Pray for insight and courage.
4. List your options, which ultimately come down to the expression of anger or the surrender of anger. (You conceivably could decide to deny the anger; it is hoped that will not be a viable option.) Weigh the advantages and disadvantages of choosing each option, as well as the advantages and disadvantages of rejecting each object. You are considering four sets of data, not two.

   Some people too readily express their anger; others too easily suppress it. Knowing your own characteristic ways of handling anger would be a consideration in reviewing your options. If you have received reliable feedback that your anger is excessive, then might this be a time for you to surrender your anger? If you are an avoider, then ought this be a time when you take the risk in asserting yourself by expressing your anger?
5. Consider which alternative seems more reasonable. Consider which alternative feels right to you. Whereas in other phases of Ignatius's rules for making a decision he uses the emotions as indicators of where the Spirit is leading, he clearly elevates reason over emotion in this step: "I must come to a decision in the matter under deliberation because of weightier motives presented to my reason, and not because of any sensual inclination."[19] If there is a discrepancy between the option that seems more reasonable and the option that feels right, then you may need further conversation with a friend.
6. This is an addition to the Ignatian steps: Ask yourself, Is the lure of God in this situation? Considering the range of possible responses I could make, what seems most life-enhancing for myself, for my community?
7. Articulate your decision and offer it to God.

Among the additional Ignatian rules for making a good choice are considering what you would advise a stranger to do in the same situation and imagining that you are on your deathbed. Ask yourself what choice you would wish you had made at this moment.

Discernment is complete when you have made a decision either to move toward an expression of your anger or to surrender your anger as an unwarranted or unnecessary response at this time.

Strategize Your Response

Plan your action, take action, evaluate your action. If necessary, go back to the drawing board and design a new plan. If you choose to surrender your anger, determine whether you need to do anything further to bring closure to your experience of anger.

Decide precisely what you will do and when you will do it. It is one thing to come clear about anger; it is another to act on that clarity. The more specific and concrete the plan, the more likely you will follow through. My impression is that many helping relationships flounder when weeks or months of insight fail to issue in workable plans with built-in accountability. Similarly, people seeking a particular change may talk at length about what they would like to see happen, but unless they design a specific plan of action, their protest can end at the discussion stage.

Making a plan reverses the cycle of anger described by Jean Baker Miller. Suppressed anger leads to frustration and inaction, resulting in feelings of weakness, decreased self-esteem, a sense of unworthiness and inferiority. Anger is thereby increased.[20] Suppressed corporate anger also leads to frustration and inaction, resulting in apathy and loss of vision. Making a plan is a strategy for reversing the cycle. The plan should include a commitment to precise action, accountability, and a timetable and plan for evaluation.

Some people who discern the need to express their anger and plan an approach will move into action, perhaps with some hesitation but with enough conviction to overcome their fear. Others discern the same need, design a reasonable plan, but are too frightened to act on that plan. Individuals may need assertiveness training before they have the sufficient assurance that they can in fact proceed. Groups surely need training in group dynamics.

In situations where the anger is the clear result of unjust or evil social structures, the plan had best include a broad base of people, well organized under effective leadership, with detailed strategies and timetables for presenting their wants and needs. Most important to the expression of anger is that, whenever possible, the anger be addressed to the person or institution immediately involved.

In dealing with an individual's anger toward another person, the formula I recommend is one broadly used in assertiveness training:

When you_____, I feel _____

because_____.

"When you . . ." names the specific, measurable behavior that provokes the anger. "I feel . . ." must also be specific—not "I feel terrible" but "I feel sad, angry, hurt." Consider the cluster of feelings and name the one that feels most apt. The "because" clause pushes the aggrieved person to name the value that is related to the offense; for example: "When you delay for several days in getting my correspondence out, I get angry. I work hard to answer letters as quickly as I can because prompt replies are important to me."

Often, role-playing the confrontation with an empathetic person enables you to take the next step. On numerous occasions, students in pastoral-care courses have role-played situations in which their anger has been either unexpressed or suppressed. They have found through the process the hope and courage to move toward a direct confrontation.

There are times when one-on-one confrontations fail repeatedly. Other strategies may be needed to bring about change. For example, two people trying to resolve conflict within an intimate relationship may get nowhere using the assertion formula. The message seems to be heard, but behaviors do not change. They may need the intervention of a professional counselor. Within work situations, after frustrated attempts to resolve an issue one on one, those in conflict may have to bring in a third person. In extremely difficult situations, coworkers may have to organize in order to have a person removed from his or her office.

The strategies needed when a group of people organize for action must be appropriate to the particular context. The last thirty years in our country have been filled with organized, grassroots protests against racism, sexism, heterosexism, militarism. Vast organizations of people account for the limited success of such movements. Many of these activities can be experienced as a corporate expression of holy anger at unjust social systems that deprive people of their civil rights. (Others, unfortunately, are organized attempts to prevent historically oppressed groups from achieving justice.)

A plan must be put in place, with the who, what, where, when, why, and how questions answered. Accountability and a method for evaluation are also needed. An individual or a group is then ready to move into action.

The relevance of taking action must not be underestimated. A study published by the American Psychological Association emphasized the importance to one's self-esteem of taking a proactive role in dealing with conflict. While the authors were not focusing explicitly on anger, they were studying the effects of coping rather than avoidance when one is faced with conflict involving anxiety and fear. The central conclusion drawn from years of research and clinical practice was as simple as this: self-esteem is achieved if a person chooses coping over avoidance when faced with conflict. If persons confront the conflict, then they feel good about themselves; if they deny or avoid the conflict, then they feel bad about themselves.[21] Furthermore, the study indicated results are not as important to self-esteem as is the fact that the person faced the conflict rather than avoided it.

What applies to self-esteem applies at least in part to anger. To be able to say, "The confrontation didn't work as I had hoped, but I feel good that I spoke up," can be at least as important as a successful outcome. However, a less-than-successful attempt to effect change may need to be followed by other attempts, in some cases more broadly based efforts with increased likelihood of success.

In the case of social anger, while the principle that the effort is more important than the outcome may apply, frustrated attempts to effect change can lead to rage rather than satisfaction. In some cases, persons may conclude that working with a justice community in itself provided a life-giving way of expressing anger. Others may resolve to continue their protest with an even stronger commitment to effect change. (I am assuming here that the cause is clearly a just one and that those involved thought carefully about the anger and planned how they wanted to initiate the confrontation. In other words, the action was considered action.)[22]

Persons interested in organizing communities to work for effective social change might use the principles and strategies of Saul Alinsky in *Rules for Radicals* and *Reveille for Radicals*.[23] Building on the perceived and expressed anger, the first task is to analyze the power structure involved and describe what outcome you most want. The outcome must be concrete, immediate, and visible. Strategizing includes finding entry points into the system needing change, assessing resources, creating allies, and taking action. Reflection and celebration follow the action.

After the action phase, evaluate to determine your level of satisfaction with your effort. A few questions will guide your assessment:

1. Were you able to communicate what you most wanted to say?
2. Was your message heard?
3. Whether or not the results of the confrontation met your hopes or expectations, are you glad that you took the action that you took?
4. How has the experience changed you?
5. Are further steps needed?

In terms of group action, the questions that may help your assessment are as follows:

1. Did we reach our goal?
2. If not, then what blocked us?
3. What changes would we make in our procedures?
4. Where do we go from here?

To summarize the three-step model for dealing with anger: Anger is a call to action, whether that action be a process of self-discovery leading to the surrender of anger or the direct expression of anger by an individual or a group. The anger must be understood, a step that often involves a person or group withdrawing for reflection and study. Discernment of God's movement in one's life and one's world allows people of faith to determine whether the expression of their anger is a holy use of energy or an effort that ought to be surrendered. If a person decides that expressing anger at this time is not the preferred choice, then an explicit articulation of that decision may help bring closure to the experience.

While in some cases the response to anger may easily be made, often the response must be more carefully planned. The plan must lead to action. Taking action is important to one's sense of self and self-esteem and crucial to the work of justice. Following the action, evaluation results in increased self-understanding, in sharper skills for using holy anger well, and in some cases, in the resolve to create a new plan.

Before concluding the chapter, I pass on to the reader a dual approach to counseling with angry individuals.

Clinical Approaches to the Treatment of Angry Individuals

Nurse psychotherapist and professor Dorothy Wilt suggests different treatment approaches for persons who have difficulty controlling anger (the anger-out group) and for persons who tend to withhold anger (the anger-in group). I call the groups *the exploders* and *the avoiders*.

Exploders need help in focusing their anger on its real source, usually their family of origin. They need assistance in developing a sense of control in enacting their anger appropriately and effectively. Because of their tendency to overreact, exploders need to focus more on their thinking process than on their feelings in order to find balance. With help they can learn calming approaches to their emotions, decreasing the ventilation of anger. Finally, they can be helped to move from overly aggressive to appropriately assertive responses.

The anger avoiders basically require the opposite approach. They need an increased awareness of their anger, as well as of other feelings. Clinicians can facilitate their experience and expression of anger within a safe environment. Avoiders need to recognize that their anger is limited and does not have to spin out of control. They can be helped to work through their guilt responses to anger and their inhibitions with regard to expressing their anger. Avoiders need assistance in learning how to nurture themselves.[24]

A Final Word

C. Welton Gaddy, in his book on coping with anger, describes the effects of unaddressed anger in a way that underscores the importance of this too often neglected emotion:

> Left alone, anger acts like a dangerous tropical depression. Mounting frustrations, disappointments, and anxieties swell normal emotional breezes into psychic blasts that threaten to devastate a person's perspective. In time, warm currents of anger intensify both in strength and heat as they swirl around inside an individual. Churning resentment combines with irrational fury. Soon, a full-blown storm with hurricane-force winds thrashes the person's well-being and lashes out at everyone and everything in the person's path. When such fully developed anger sweeps across the landscape of an individual's life, the wreckage is usually so pervasive that good intentions, noble goals, and helpful relationships lie in ruins right alongside all that is bad.[25]

Every surge of anger has a message to convey: about oneself, about relationships, about hopes and dreams, about social justice, about the lure of God in one's life. Not every message will be heard, in some situations because other voices speak more urgently. If some of the messages are deciphered some of the time and action is taken accordingly, then one can discover in oneself and offer to the world holy anger, enacted in faith and hope and love.

Epilogue

Befriend your anger. Then can you hear the deeper truth that anger is revealing. Sometimes anger tiptoes, a gentle wake-up call slipping into consciousness and building, building, building. "I think I'm getting angry about this . . ."

Sometimes anger's ring is musical—a clock radio with a snooze alarm to let you slowly rise to the brightness of its day. "Maybe I am angry. Maybe I'm just tired."

Sometimes the sound's a deafening clang—a jolt that throws you out of bed.

Befriend your anger. Only then can you decide the what and when and how of your reply.

Befriend your anger. Learn to stay with it, to play with it, to leap back to its roots. There you'll find a child in fear and pain . . . return, an adult with compassion.

Befriend your anger. When you feel the sting of others' hurt, welcome the anger of hope: holy energy stirring in your soul, the work of Jesus in a hostile world—atonement.

Befriend your godlike anger, and be at peace.

From the creation of humankind to the end time, anger is a fact of life, of God's life and of the life of those made in God's image. Difficult, painful, confounding, energizing, always challenging, anger is complex and multivalent. Each person is called to probe the complexities of anger even while probing God's energy as discovered in all intense emotion. The task is to speak the anger of hope clearly and directly, lest it become the anger of despair.

This book has looked long and hard at the origin of anger in infancy, the pathways of anger through the life cycle, and the biblical revelation about the anger of God, the anger of Jesus, and human anger. My effort has also been to design useful strategies for assessing anger and for responding in ways that result in more honest, just living. The Sunday brunch model for dealing with anger hopefully has something for every taste.

My wish and my prayer is that people of faith find faith enough in themselves and in their emotional lives to befriend and use their anger well. Both individually and collectively angry people often have the power to change their lives and to effect change for the sake of their neighbor— that is, to use to the best of one's possibilities "the power of anger in the work of love."[1]

Notes

Preface

1. Don M. Wardlaw, "Preaching from Anger," *Living Pulpit* 2, 4 (Oct.–Dec. 1993): 36.
2. Ibid., 37.
3. Ibid.

Introduction: A Call to Understanding

1. For a fuller discussion of the defenses against anger, see Daniel J. Heinrichs, "A Psychoanalytic Approach to Anger Management Training," *Journal of Psychology and Christianity* 5, 4 (1986): 12–23.
2. P. David Finks, *The Radical Vision of Saul Alinsky* (New York: Paulist Press, 1984), 141.
3. Jean Baker Miller, "The Construction of Anger in Women and Men," in Judith V. Jordan, Janet L. Surrey, and Alexandra G. Kaplan, eds., *Women's Growth in Connection* (New York: Guilford Press, 1991), 182.
4. Women-Church groups have grown up across the country and in many parts of the world. At Women-Church, women gather to share their faith and their lives through potluck meals and creative, life-giving worship. For a further description of Women-Church, see Mary E. Hunt, "Defining Women-Church," *Waterwheel: A Quarterly Newsletter of the Women's Alliance for Theology, Ethics, and Ritual*, 3, 2 (summer 1990): 1–2; see also Rosemary Radford Ruether, *Women-Church: Theology and Practice of Feminist Liturgical Communities* (San Francisco: Harper & Row, 1985).
5. Miller, "Construction of Anger," 182.
6. Carol E. Franz and Kathleen M. White, "Individuation and Attachment in Personality Development: Extending Erikson's Theory," in Abigail Stewart and Brinton Lykes, eds., *Gender and Personality: Current Perspectives on Theory and Research* (Durham, N.C.: Duke University Press, 1985), 136–68.

1. The Complexity of Anger

1. Thomas Aquinas, *Summa Theologiae*, 1, 2, q.23, a.3c; cited in Mary Daly, *Pure Lust: Elemental Feminist Philosophy* (Boston: Beacon Press, 1984), 370.

2. Daly, *Pure Lust*, 370.

3. This is a revised and expanded version of the reasons that anger is a difficult emotion, published in Carroll Saussy, "Anger, a Mixed Emotion," *Living Pulpit* 2, 4 (Oct.–Dec. 1993): 38–39.

4. For a helpful treatment of the emotions, particularly anger, shame, and guilt, see James D. Whitehead and Evelyn Eaton Whitehead, *Shadows of the Heart: A Spirituality of the Negative Emotions* (New York: Crossroad, 1994).

5. Abraham Maslow, *Toward a Psychology of Being*, rev. ed. (Princeton, N.J.: D. Van Nostrand, 1968).

6. The expressions *true self* and *false self* are developed in Alice Miller, *The Drama of the Gifted Child* (New York: Basic Books, 1981).

7. Nico Frijda, "The Laws of Emotion," *American Psychologist* 43, 5 (May 1988): 349–58.

8. Ibid., 351.

9. Don E. Saliers, *The Soul in Paraphrase: Prayer and the Religious Affections* (New York: Seabury Press, 1980), 15–18. See also John A. Struzzo, "Anger: Destructive and Life-Giving Energy," in Brendan P. Riordan, ed., *Anger: Issues of Emotional Living in an Age of Stress for Clergy and Religious* (Whitinsville, Mass.: Affirmation Books, 1985), 116–31. Struzzo distinguishes feeling (inner experience of energy) from emotions (reactive process or outward expression of feeling).

10. C. D. Spielberger, G. Jacobs, S. Russell, S. Crane, and R. J. Crane, "Assessment of Anger: The State–Trait Anger Scale," in J. N. Butcher and C. D. Spielberger, eds., *Advances in Personality Assessment* (Hillsdale, N.J.: Erlbaum, 1983), 2: 161–89; cited in Sandra Thomas, ed., *Women and Anger* (New York: Springer, 1993), 40–42.

11. Miriam D. Ukeritis, "Anger on Behalf of Justice," in Riordan, ed., *Anger*, 140.

12. Carol Tavris, *Anger: The Misunderstood Emotion*, rev. ed. (New York: Simon & Schuster, 1989).

13. Andrew Lester, *Coping with Your Anger: A Christian Guide* (Philadelphia: Westminster Press, 1983). See also Daniel G. Bagby, *Understanding Anger in the Church* (Nashville: Broadman Press, 1979), 22–23.

14. Audre Lorde (*Sister Outsider* [Trumansburg, N.Y.: Crossing Press, 1984], 129) says that "hatred is the fury of those who do not share our goals, and its object is death and destruction. Anger is a grief of distortions between persons, and its object is change." At the same time she recognizes that anger and cruelty are by-products of hatred.

15. See Ronald T. Potter-Efron and Patricia S. Potter-Efron, *Anger, Alcoholism, and Addiction: Treating Individuals, Couples, and Families*, (New York: W. W. Norton, 1991), 4–5. The authors distinguish among anger (an emotional state), rage (the strongest form of anger), aggression (which they define as behavior intended to harm), hostility (an attitude that sees others as enemy), resentment (the opposite of forgiveness), hatred (the unchanging dislike of another). However,

as discussed in the next section of this chapter, Kathleen Greider offers a far more promising and challenging understanding of aggression.

16. David Blumenthal, *Facing the Abusing God: A Theology of Protest* (Louisville: Westminster/John Knox Press, 1993), 65.

17. Kathleen J. Greider, " 'Too Militant?': Aggression, Gender and the Construction of Justice," *School of Theology at Claremont (Calif.) Occasional Paper* 3, 2 (April 1993): 1–8.

18. Ibid., 2.

19. Eugene H. Peterson, "A Pastor's Quarrel with God," *Princeton Seminary Bulletin*, 11, 3 (1990): 271.

20. Greider, " 'Too Militant?' " 3.

21. Potter-Efron and Potter-Efron, *Anger, Alcoholism, and Addiction.* The authors believe that expressing anger "prevents physical and emotional collapse, preserving a capacity for the eventual experience of other emotions when those can be more safely expressed" (34).

22. Tavris, *Anger*, 88–89.

23. Speaking specifically of anger, Nico Frijda makes what I consider both an overstatement and an accurate human reaction to hurt: "For someone who is truly angry, the thing that happened is felt to be absolutely bad. It is disgraceful. It is not merely a disgraceful act but one that flows from the actor's very nature and disposition. Somebody who has acted so disgracefully *is* disgraceful and thus will always be. The offense and the misery it causes have a character of perpetuity" (Frijda, "Laws," 354).

24. Ibid., 350.

25. Alastair Campbell, *The Gospel of Anger* (London: SPCK, 1986), 52.

26. Potter-Efron and Potter-Efron describe the management of anger in anger-avoidant families. Members have difficulty asking directly for what they want. They hint at needs, demonstrate both passive–aggressive and martyr behavior, and bury their resentment. Anger-avoidant families often use "stuff and blow" patterns of behavior. The right to express anger may be given to the more or most powerful member of the family. See Potter-Efron and Potter-Efron, *Anger, Alcoholism, and Addiction*, 53–54.

27. Alice Miller, *For Your Own Good: Hidden Cruelty in Child-Rearing and the Roots of Violence*, trans. Hildegarde Hannum and Hunter Hannum (New York: Farrar, Straus & Giroux, 1983). See also Alice Miller, *Thou Shalt Not Be Aware: Society's Betrayal of the Child* (New York: Farrar, Straus & Giroux, 1984).

28. Lenore E. Auerbach Walker and Angela Browne, "Gender and Victimization by Intimates," in Abigail Stewart and Brinton Lykes, eds., *Gender and Personality: Current Perspectives on Theory and Research* (Durham, N.C.: Duke University Press, 1985), 91–107.

29. Leslie Brody, "Gender Differences in Emotional Development: A Review of Theories and Research," in Stewart and Lykes, eds., *Gender and Personality*, 50.

30. Another study notes that girls' angry expressions decreased sharply at age two. Psychoanalytic, genetic-evolutionary, and sociological theories predict that "women should experience and express less anger and guilt than do men; experience and express more self-directed hostility, envy, shame, depression,

vulnerability, helplessness, and anxiety than do men; direct feelings internally rather than externally; be more sensitive to nonverbal cues than are men; and be more emotionally expressive in general than are men" (Ibid., 24).

31. James R. Averill and W. Douglas Frost, "Differences between Men and Women in the Everyday Experience of Anger," in James R. Averill, *Anger and Aggression: An Essay in Emotion* (New York: Springer, 1982), 281–316.

32. Harriet Goldhor Lerner, *The Dance of Anger* (New York: Harper & Row, 1985).

33. Tavrls, *Anger*, 207.

34. June Crawford, Susan Kippax, Jenny Onyx, Una Gault, and Pan Benton, *Emotion and Gender: Constructing Meaning from Memory* (London: SAGE Publications, 1992), 180, 182.

35. Ibid., 182.

36. Luise Eichenbaum and Susie Orback, *Understanding Women: A Feminist Psychoanalytic Approach* (New York: Basic Books, 1983), 189.

37. Lorde, *Sister Outsider*, 145.

38. Dale Russakoff, "Lani Guinier Is Still Alive and Talking," *Washington Post Magazine* (December 12, 1993): 15–19, 32–35.

39. The definition of *han* is attributed to Hyun Young Hak in Chung Hyun Kyung, *Struggle to Be the Sun Again: Introducing Asian Women's Theology* (Maryknoll, N.Y.: Orbis Books, 1991), 42.

40. Ibid.

2. The Origin and Development of Anger

1. The term *boarder babies* refers to children who are unable to leave the hospital with their parent(s) for social-emotional reasons.

2. Daniel J. Heinrichs, "A Psychoanalytic Approach to Anger Management Training," *Journal of Psychology and Christianity* 5, 4 (1986): 12.

3. Donald Nathanson, *Shame and Pride: Affect, Sex, and the Birth of the Self* (New York: W. W. Norton, 1992). Nathanson holds that the primitive affects, listed in two-word groups wherein each indicates a mild and intense form of the affect, are interest–excitement, enjoyment–joy, surprise–startle, fear–terror, distress–anguish, anger-rage.

4. See Thomas Gordon, *Parent Effectiveness Training* (New York: Wyden, 1970); and Paula Caplan, *Don't Blame Mother* (New York: Harper & Row, 1989), 25.

5. See Judith V. Jordan, Janet L. Surrey, and Alexandra G. Kaplan, eds., *Women's Growth in Connection* (New York: Guilford Press, 1991). Written by feminist writers at the Stone Center in Wellesley, Massachusetts, the collection expands on the work of the British object relations theorists. Contributor Janet Surrey believes that object relations should be called subject relations and that separation–individuation should be called relationship–differentiation; see her chapter "The 'Self-in-Relation': A Theory of Women's Development," 36.

6. Sandra P. Thomas, ed., *Women and Anger* (New York: Springer, 1993), 33.

7. Michael E. Kerr and Murray Bowen, *Family Evaluation: An Approach Based on Bowen Theory* (New York: W. W. Norton, 1988).

8. The work of Nancy Chodorow triggered my conversion from a conviction that women are the natural caregivers to the realization that patriarchy has given women that assignment; see Nancy Chodorow, *The Reproduction of Mothering: Psychoanalysis and the Sociology of Mothering* (Berkeley: University of California Press, 1978). See also Jordan et al., *Women's Growth*.

9. See Edward P. Wimberly, "Minorities," in Robert J. Wicks, Richard D. Parsons, and Donald Capps, eds., *Clinical Handbook for Pastoral Care and Counseling*, expanded ed. (New York: Paulist Press, 1993), 1:305–7. See also Monica McGoldrick, "Ethnicity, Cultural Diversity and Normality," in Froma Walsh, ed., *Normal Family Processes*, 2d ed. (New York: Guilford Press, 1993), 354. McGoldrick refers to studies on male–female roles in black families, as well as studies indicating that black fathers take a larger part in housekeeping and child-rearing than do white fathers.

10. Froma Walsh, "Conceptualization of Normal Family Processes," in idem, ed., *Normal Family Processes*, 15.

11. Pamela D. Couture, "The Family Policy Debate: A Feminist Theologian's Response," *Journal of Pastoral Theology* 3 (summer 1993): 78.

12. Patricia H. Davis, "Women and the Burden of Empathy," *Journal of Pastoral Theology* 3 (summer 1993): 29–38.

13. Ibid., 30.

14. Building on Jean Baker Miller's term *being-in-relation* and Janet Surrey's *self-in-relation*, the anger of hope might be called *separation-in-relation anger*. See Jean Baker Miller, "The Development of Women's Sense of Self," in Jordan et al., *Women s Growth*, 11; and Janet Surrey, "The 'Self-in-Relation.'"

15. Following the line of thought in the preceding note, such anger might also be called *abandonment-in-relation anger*.

16. John Bowlby, *Separation: Anxiety and Anger* (New York: Basic Books, 1973), 56.

17. Ibid., 250.

18. Judith Duerk, *Circle of Stones: Woman's Journey to Herself* (San Diego: Lura Media, 1990), 30.

19. Luise Eichenbaum, and Susie Orback, *Understanding Women: A Feminist Psychoanalytic Approach* (Basic Books, 1983), 150–51.

20. Alice Miller, *For Your Own Good: Hidden Cruelty in Child-Rearing and the Roots of Violence*, trans. Hildegarde Hannum and Hunter Hannum (New York: Farrar, Straus & Giroux, 1983), 106. Miller goes on to say that this refusal can lead to suicide and drug addiction. See also idem, *Thou Shalt Not Be Aware: Society's Betrayal of the Child* (New York: Farrar, Straus & Giroux, 1984).

21. Thomas, *Women and Anger*, 36.

22. Alice Miller, *The Drama of the Gifted Child: How Narcissistic Parents Form and Deform the Emotional Lives of Their Talented Children* (New York: Basic Books, 1981), 6.

23. Carl Rogers, "My Philosophy of Interpersonal Relations and How It Grew," in Hung Min Chiang and Abraham Maslow, eds., *The Healthy Personality*, 2d. ed. (New York: D. Van Nostrand, 1977), 25–26.

24. Lloyd DeMause, "The Universality of Incest," *Journal of Psychohistory* 19, 2 (fall 1991): 125; original italics removed.

25. Ibid., 136. This data was included in a workshop panel presentation by psychologist Bruno Heidik that was titled "International Consultation on Sexual Abuse and Power in Cross Cultural Perspective" (presented to the American Association of Pastoral Counselors convention, Louisville, Ky., April 16, 1993).

26. Statistic supplied to the author by Frank Molony, assistant state's attorney, Montgomery County, Maryland.

3. Anger and the Life Cycle

1. Hugh Cleary, "Dynamics of Power and Anger," *New Blackfriars* 72 (fall 1991): 79–88. For a complete discussion of Erik Erikson's eight ages, see Erik Erikson, *Childhood and Society* (New York: W. W. Norton, 1963).

2. Donald Capps, "Pastoral Care and the Eight Deadly Vices," *Pastoral Psychology* 32, 1 (fall 1983): 8–23.

3. Lyn Mikel Brown and Carol Gilligan, *Meeting at the Crossroads: Women's Psychology and Girls' Development* (Cambridge, Mass.: Harvard University Press, 1992).

4. Carol Gilligan believes Erikson sees attachment as an impediment to individuation or separateness; see her *In a Different Voice: Psychological Theory and Women's Development* (Cambridge, Mass.: Harvard University Press, 1982), 12–13. Her claim is that, across cultures, women define themselves in relation and connection to other people more than men do. Consequently, "male gender identity is threatened by intimacy while female gender identity is threatened by separation. Thus males tend to have difficulty with relationships, while females tend to have problems with individuation" (8).

5. Carol E. Franz and Kathleen M. White, "Individuation and Attachment in Personality Development: Extending Erikson's Theory," in Abigail Stewart and Brinton Lykes, eds., *Gender and Personality: Current Perspectives on Theory and Research* (Durham, N.C.: Duke University Press, 1985), 136.

6. Erikson discussed the centrality of generativity to his thinking in an informal conversation with students from the Graduate Theological Union, Berkeley, California, 1976.

7. Honesty versus suppression might best be placed on the individuation path. My interest, however, is in honest relationship. As the paths are currently designed, honest expression of feeling seems to fit better with empathy and collaboration than with industry; suppression, with excessive caution or power than with inferiority.

8. Franz and White, "Individuation," 146.

9. C. D. Schneider, "Shame," in Rodney J. Hunter, ed., *Dictionary of Pastoral Care and Counseling* (Nashville: Abingdon Press, 1990), 1160.

10. Audre Lorde, *Sister Outsider* (Trumansburg, N.Y.: Crossing Press, 1984), 146.

11. Schneider, "Shame," 1160.

12. Norman Cousins, *Anatomy of an Illness* (Boston: G. K. Hall, 1980).

13. Gabriele Rico, *Pain and Possibility: Writing Your Way through Personal Crisis* (Los Angeles: Jeremy P. Tarcher, 1991), 210.

14. Brown and Gilligan, *Meeting*, 45.

15. Ibid., 47–48.

16. Ibid., 48.

17. Ibid., 164.

18. Ibid., 97.

19. Ibid., 61.

20. Ibid., 4.

21. Mary Daly, *Pure Lust: Elemental Feminist Philosophy* (Boston: Beacon Press, 1984), 370.

22. Brown and Gilligan, *Meeting*, 214–15.

23. Ibid., 230.

24. The following account is taken from Graciela Sevilla, "Fresh Pain from an Old Wound: Arrest Triggers Memory of Girlhood Rape," *Washington Post*, 29 December 1993, Maryland final edition 1, 12.

25. I am indebted to Dr. Natalie O'Byrne, former consultant at the Lloyd Center Counseling Service of San Francisco Theological Seminary, San Anselmo, California, for sharing her understanding of this dynamic.

26. John Bowlby, *Separation*, 249.

27. Daly, *Pure Lust*, 370.

4. God's Anger: How One Question Became Three

1. The tradition has also developed theologies of God that place God beyond emotion, believing that emotion would be a sign of mutability and dependence in God. This discussion stays with biblical testimony and does not discuss the variety of interpretations of God's emotions put forward by systematic theologians over the centuries.

2. Bruce Edward Baloian, *Anger in the Old Testament* (New York: Peter Lang, 1992), 5–7. Baloian finds 518 references to the anger of God in the Hebrew Bible, which include ten Hebrew words for anger. Christian ethicist Alastair Campbell claims there are over 400 references to anger in the Hebrew Bible (with twenty-nine references to God's anger across the Gospels, epistles, and apocalyptic literature). See Alastair Campbell, *The Gospel of Anger* (London: SPCK, 1986), 5–7.

3. George M. Landes, "Some Biblical and Theological Reflections on the Wrath of God," *Living Pulpit* 2, 4 (Oct.–Dec. 1993): 10–11.

4. David R. Blumenthal, *Facing the Abusing God: A Theology of Protest* (Louisville: Westminster John Knox Press, 1993), 242.

5. Alastair Campbell provides a context in which one can place God's anger. He traces six main themes that describe God's power, three of them related to a destructive God, three to a creative God: demon, tempter, avenger, and lover, servant, savior. Campbell notes the claim of P. Volz (*Das Damonische in Jahwe*, 1924) that monotheism had to incorporate primitive elements of God, "notably the unpredictable and frightening demons of the desert night and the gods of wind, storm, earthquake and fire (Isaiah 66,15; Jeremiah 23,19, Numbers 16, 1–35 and 11, 1–3)" (Campbell, *Gospel*, 34, 36).

6. Blumenthal, *Facing*, 220.

7. Joanne Carlson Brown and Rebecca Parker, "For God So Loved the World?" in Joanne Carlson Brown and Carole R. Bohn, eds., *Christianity,*

Patriarchy, and Abuse: A Feminist Critique (Cleveland: Pilgrim Press, 1989), 2. See also James Poling, *The Abuse of Power: A Theological Problem* (Nashville: Abingdon Press, 1991).

8. Brown and Parker, "For God So Loved," 26.

9. James D. Whitehead and Evelyn Eaton Whitehead, "Christians and Their Passions," *Warren Lecture Series in Catholic Studies* 21 (September 27, 1992): 3.

10. Campbell, *Gosepl*, 3–4, 40.

11. Alice Miller, *For Your Own Good: Hidden Cruelty in Child-Rearing and the Roots of Violence*, trans. Hildegarde Hannum and Hunter Hannum (New York: Farrar, Straus & Giroux, 1983).

12. Walter Brueggemann, *Old Testament Theology: Essays on Structure, Theme, and Text*, ed. Patrick D. Miller (Minneapolis: Fortress Press, 1992), 18–52.

13. Ibid., 25.

14. Ibid., 19.

15. Blumenthal, *Facing*, 109.

16. Carol Tavris (*Anger: The Misunderstood Emotion*, rev. ed. [New York: Simon & Schuster, 1989], 211) cites the research of Mary Kay Biaggio. Biaggio found that while men get angry, women feel hurt. Women blame themselves, feel ambivalent about expressing anger; men focus on hostility and blame the other.

17. Perhaps the whole epistle to the Romans is an attempt to make sense of the crucifixion: "The wrath of God is revealed" (1:18). None is righteous; all deserve to be destroyed. The epistle orders chaos through a detailed theology of law.

18. Whitehead and Whitehead, "Christians," 3.

5. Jesus' Anger

1. Garry Wills, Outlook: "Women Priests? The Gospel Truth: So Sayeth the Lord to the Pope," *Washington Post*, June 5, 1994.

2. I have chosen to use the Markan account in 8:27–30. See also Matt. 16:12–20 and Luke 9:18–20.

3. Some of the ideas in this exploration of the question "Who do you say that I am?" first appeared in Carroll Saussy, "Pastoral Implications," *Lectionary Homiletics* 1, 5, (April 1990), 3, 9–10, 15–16, 21–22, 27.

4. Carroll Saussy, *God Images and Self Esteem: Empowering Women in a Patriarchal Society* (Louisville: Westminster John Knox Press, 1991), 60.

5. Rosemary Radford Ruether, *Sexism and God-Talk: Toward A Feminist Theology* (Boston: Beacon Press, 1983), 66. See also Elisabeth Schüssler Fiorenza, *In Memory of Her: A Feminist Theological Reconstruction of Christian Origins* (New York: Crossroad, 1983), 147, 151. Fiorenza discusses the liberation from the patriarchal family structure within the Jesus movement. The saying of Jesus in Mark 3:35 claims that those who live God's goodness constitute Jesus' true family. Notice that brothers, sisters, and mothers are singled out in the verse, but not fathers. There is but one father in this family.

6. Rita Nakashima Brock, *Journeys by Heart: A Christology of Erotic Power* (New York: Crossroad, 1988).

7. Fiorenza argues a progression from a more charismatic form of leadership to a more hierarchical form. Church historian and seminary professor Ted Campbell is convinced that hierarchical forms of leadership prevailed in most

churches by the end of the second century, roughly 170–180. He believes there were both hierarchical and charismatic forms of leadership early on, and by the 170s and 180s, the hierarchical forms had prevailed. See Ted A. Campbell, "Charismata in the Christian Communities of the Second Century," *Wesleyan Theological Journal* 17, 2 (fall 1982): 7–25.

8. Fiorenza, *In Memory*, 235–36.

9. Rosemary Radford Ruether, "A Feminist Critique and Reconstruction of Christology" (address given at the conference "Images of Christ through the Eyes of Women," Trinity College, Washington, D.C., November 18, 1993).

10. Justo Gonzalez, *The Story of Christianity* (San Francisco: Harper & Row, 1984), 1:158–67.

11. Ibid., 1:164–66.

12. Ruether, "Feminist Critique."

13. Jean Danielou, *The Lord of History* (Chicago: Henry Regnery, 1958); cited in Vincent Zamoyta, ed., *A Theology of Christ: Sources* (Milwaukee: Bruce, 1967), 200.

14. Bonnie S. Anderson and Judith P. Zinsser, *A History of Their Own: Women in Europe from Prehistory to the Present* (New York: Harper & Row, 1988), 1:183, 190–91.

15. Chung Hyun Kyung, *Struggle to Be the Sun Again: Introducing Asian Women's Theology* (Maryknoll, N.Y.: Orbis Books, 1991), 61.

16. Joanne Carlson Brown and Rebecca Parker, eds., *Christianity, Patriarchy and Abuse: A Feminist Critique* (Cleveland: Pilgrim Press, 1989), 2.

17. For a discussion of the ways in which Jesus threatened the powerful, see Irene Foulkes, "Bible and Tradition," *Mid Stream* 21 (July 1982): 338–49.

18. Rita Nakashima Brock, "On Losing Your Innocence" (address given at the conference "Images of Christ through the Eyes of Women," Trinity College, Washington, D.C., November 18, 1993).

19. From an unpublished sermon of Carter Heyward; cited in Jacquelyn Grant, *White Women's Christ and Black Women's Jesus: Feminist Christology and Womanist Response* (Atlanta: Scholars Press, 1989), 187.

20. See Gail R. O'Day, "John," in Carol A. Newsom and Sharon H. Ringe, eds., *The Women's Bible Commentary* (Louisville: Westminster John Knox Press, 1992), 293.

21. This Gospel scene is discussed in Carroll Saussy and Barbara Clarke, "The Healing Power of Anger," in Jeanne Stevenson Moessner, ed., *Woman-Care* (Minneapolis: Fortress Press, forthcoming).

22. Bruce J. Malina and Richard L. Rohrbaugh, *Social Science Commentary on the Synoptic Gospels* (Minneapolis: Fortress Press, 1992), 249. The authors say, "In the central episode (bracketed by the fig tree stories) Jesus' behavior is directed at people who performed a legitimate function in the Temple, enabling the performance of proper sacrifice commanded by God in the torah. To drive them away is equivalent to putting a halt to such divinely willed temple sacrifice. It is also a serious honor challenge to the Temple authorities" (250).

23. Ched Myers, *Binding the Strong Man: A Political Reading of Mark's Story of Jesus* (Maryknoll, N.Y.: Orbis Books, 1988), 297–98.

24. W. Telford, *The Barren Temple and the Withered Tree: A Redactionist-Critical Analysis of the Cursing of the Fig-Tree Pericope in Mark's Gospel and Its*

Relation to the Cleansing of the Temple Tradition (Sheffield, England: JSOT Press, 1980), 196; cited in Myers, *Binding the Strong Man*, 298. Myers adds, "The symbolic action of Jesus' cursing of the fig tree is Mark's own little haggadic tale, as well as a midrash on Hosea 9:16. Its narrative function is to begin Jesus' ideological project of subverting the temple-centered social order. The reappearance of the fig tree in the apocalyptic parable (13:28–32) at the conclusion to this section confirms this. In the second sermon, the leafy (i.e., fruitless) fig tree is offered as a sign of the 'end time.' The world that is coming to an end is the world of the temple-based state" (299).

25. "The reader must choose which reality to believe in: the temple-as-withered-to-the-root (sign of a system that is coming to an end) or the temple-as-bigger-than-life (sign of a system that will never end)" (Telford, *Barren Temple*, 196, quoted in Myers, *Binding the Strong Man*, 298.)

26. Alastair Campbell, *The Gospel of Anger* (London: SPCK, 1986), 98–99.

6. Human Anger

1. D. Cameron Murchison, Jr., "Anger and the Praise of God," *Journal for Preachers*, 9, 2 (1986): 4–5.

2. Dominic Crossan notes that the present form of this narrative was "rewritten to show in ideal fashion how the ideal community of Israel should act in face of such a crime." Crossan's commentary focuses on its tribal significance; he says nothing about the murder of the concubine. Dominic M. Crossan, OSM, "Judges," in *The Jerome Biblical Commentary* I (Englewood Cliffs, N.J.: Prentice-Hall, 1968), 161–62.

3. Phyllis Trible, *Texts of Terror: Literary Feminist Readings of Biblical Narratives* (Philadelphia: Fortress Press, 1984), 66.

4. Keith A. Russell, "Prophetic Anger from the Perspective of Jeremiah," *Living Pulpit* 2, 4 (Oct.–Dec. 1993): 13.

5. See Denise Dombkowski Hopkins, *Journey Through the Psalms: A Path to Wholeness* (New York: United Church Press, 1990).

6. David Blumenthal, *Facing The Abusing God: A Theology of Protest* (Louisville: Westminster John Knox Press, 1993), 144.

7. I recognize a double standard I bring to the Bible. I affirm the candid anger expressed in violent language in the lament psalms. The cry of the psalmist is a legitimate, even holy, expression of human rage at loss. People of faith echo these cries whether the pain suffered be the result of death, of accident, or the unnecessary pain suffered because of injustice or cruelty.

However, I deny that God would express anger in the same violent language or use the same physical threats or curses. When God is described as the one who will behave viciously toward God's enemies I lean toward David Blumenthal's conclusion that such a God is abusive. Because God does not share the limits of human life, God has no need to project anger onto humankind the way humans need to project their anger onto God. God does not need to crush the sinner. Perhaps I expect God to feel pain and anger in the presence of suffering and injustice, but without retaliating in word or deed.

8. Andrew Lester, *Coping with Your Anger: A Christian Guide* (Philadelphia: Westminster Press, 1983), 45.

9. The seven deadly sins are pride, envy, anger, sloth, avarice, gluttony, and lust. See D. Cameron Murchison, Jr., "Anger and the Praise of God," *Journal for Preachers* 9, 2 (1986): 2–7.

10. Gustav Stählin, "The Wrath of Man and the Wrath of God in the New Testament," *Theological Dictionary of the New Testament*, Gerhard Friedrich, ed., Grand Rapids, Mich.: Wm. B. Eerdmans Publishing Co., 1967), 5:419.

11. Stephen W. Hinks, "Anger—What Does the Bible Say?" *Journal of Christian Education, Papers 86* (July 1986): 37.

12. John M. Court, "On the Expression of Anger: A Response," *Journal of Christian Education, Papers 86* (July 1986): 43–45.

13. Charles E. Cerling, "Some Thoughts on a Biblical View of Anger: A Response," *Journal of Psychology and Theology* 2 (1974): 267.

14. Valerie Saiving, "The Human Situation: A Feminine View," in Carol P. Christ and Judith Plaskow, *Womanspirit Rising: A Feminist Reader in Religion* (San Francisco: Harper & Row, 1979), 25–42. Originally published in *Journal of Religion* 40, (April 1960): 100–112.

Conclusion: A Call to Faithful Action

1. Ronald T. Potter-Efron and Patricia S. Potter-Efron point out that chronically angry persons are oversensitive to cues in their environment. Such persons give impulsive, exaggerated responses; experience an anger rush after the action; and are unable to withdraw (*Anger, Alcoholism, and Addiction: Treating Individuals, Couples, and Families* [New York: W. W. Norton, 1991], 40). Potter-Efron and Potter-Efron offer a helpful anger inventory and assessment form. The range of handling anger includes anger avoidance, explosive anger, manipulative anger, resentment, moral anger, shame-based anger, envy and jealousy, excitatory anger or addictive anger, and habitual anger (83). See also Sandra P. Thomas, *Women and Anger* (New York: Springer, 1993), for treatment approaches.

2. Potter-Efron and Potter-Efron (*Anger, Alcoholism, and Addiction*) outline three schools of thought in approaches to anger: ventilationist, reductionist, and management. Each one is useful for some population. See also the gestalt process found in E. Polster and M. Polster, *Gestalt Therapy Integrated* (New York: Brunner/ Mazel, 1973); J. Zinker, *Creative Process in Gestalt Therapy* (New York: Brunner/ Mazel, 1977). Potter-Efron and Potter-Efron summarize the gestalt sequence: "(1) an initial *awareness* of a sensation, emotion, or thought; (2) an *excitement* stage that serves to focus a person's attention upon the particular issue; (3) an *action* stage during which the excitement is transformed into behavior; (4) a *contact* stage that gives the person both internal and external feedback on those actions, and (5) a *withdrawal* stage, in which the person withdraws energy and interest from that concern and goes on to something else (a new awareness)" (*Anger, Alcoholism, and Addiction*, 31–32).

3. Denise Dombkowski Hopkins, *Journey through the Psalms: A Path to Wholeness* (New York: United Church Press, 1990), 93.

4. Carol B. Wilson has asked that her full name be used in this book.

5. Kathleen Fischer and Thomas Hart provide prayers and rituals for both caregivers and those seeking their help in dealing with anger in *A Counselor's Prayer Book* (New York: Paulist Press, 1994).

6. William J. Gaultiere, "A Biblical Perspective on Therapeutic Treatment of Client Anger at God," *Journal of Psychology and Christianity* 8 (1989): 44.

7. Clinician Sharon Cheston suggests specific steps for staying with an experience of anger. She encourages clients to sit still and feel their anger. As persons sit with their anger, it waxes. When the feeling peaks, she has them breathe slowly and then emote by crying, yelling, or pounding a pillow. Cheston supports their justifiable anger, allowing clients to continue expressing it "until they become exhausted and the feeling wanes. Clients will feel tired but relieved" (Sharon E. Cheston, "Counseling Adult Survivors of Childhood Sexual Abuse," in Robert J. Wicks and Richard D. Parsons, eds., *Clinical Handbook of Pastoral Counseling* [New York: Paulist Press, 1993], 2: 476).

8. John A. Struzzo, "Anger: Destructive and Life-Giving Energy," in Brendan P. Riordan, ed., *Anger: Issues of Emotional Living in an Age of Stress for Clergy and Religious* (Whitinsville, Mass.: Affirmation Books, 1985), 118.

9. John Patton, *Is Human Forgiveness Possible? A Pastoral Care Perspective* (Nashville: Abingdon Press, 1985), 141.

10. This suggestion is an adaptation of a method employed by the Harvard research team in their work with adolescent girls. Conversations between researchers and students were taped, then played four times in a effort to understand the pressures and struggles of adolescence for girls. See Lyn Mikel Brown and Carol Gilligan, *Meeting at the Crossroads: Women's Psychology and Girls' Development* (Cambridge, Mass.: Harvard University Press, 1982), 25–31.

11. Gabriele Lusser Rico, *Writing the Natural Way* (Los Angeles: Jeremy P. Tarcher, 1983).

12. Albert Ellis, *Anger, How to Live with and without It* (New York: Citadel Press, 1977).

13. Ira Progoff, *At a Journal Workshop: The Basic Text and Guide for Using the Intensive Journal* (New York: Dialogue House, 1975).

14. The ideas were sparked by Rodney L. Bassett, et al., "Righteous and Sinful Anger from the Perspectives of Christian Therapists and College Students," *Journal of Psychology and Christianity* 8, 3 (fall 1989): 47–56.

15. Potter-Efron and Potter-Efron suggest a plan for keeping an anger-cycle diary in *Anger, Alcoholism, and Addiction*, 44.

16. William R. Miller and Kathleen A. Jackson, *Practical Psychology for Pastors* (Englewood Cliffs, N.J.: Prentice-Hall, 1985), 248.

17. Louis J. Puhl, *The Spiritual Exercises of St. Ignatius: A New Translation Based on Studies in the Language of the Autograph* (Westminster, Md.: Newman Press, 1962). There are several reasons why I am hesitant to recommend the *Exercises*. Primarily, I find it difficult to appreciate Ignatius's worldview; he operates out of a cosmology that is filled with demons. More seriously, he casts woman in demonic terms; for example: "The enemy conducts himself as a woman. He is a weakling before a show of strength, and a tyrant if he has his will. It is characteristic of a woman in a quarrel with a man to lose courage and take to flight if the man shows that he is determined and fearless. However, if the man loses courage and begins to flee, the anger, vindictiveness, and rage of the woman surge up and know no bounds. In the same way, the enemy becomes weak, loses courage, and turns to flight with his seductions as soon as one leading a spiritual life faces his

NOTES

155

temptations boldly, and does exactly opposite of what he suggests. However, if one begins to be afraid and to lose courage in temptations, no wild animal on earth can be more fierce than the enemy of our human nature. He will carry out his perverse intentions with consummate malice" (145).

18. Ibid., 71–78.

19. Ibid., 76. These are the rules for the third phase of making a decision. The first centers directly on one's divine vocation; the second attends to consolation versus desolation in prayer when one is tentatively dealing with the choice. In the third phase, reason provides the major guidance.

20. Jean Baker Miller, "The Construction of Anger in Women and Men," in Judith V. Jordan, Janet L. Surrey, and Alexandra G. Kaplan, eds., *Women's Growth in Connection* (New York: Guilford Press, 1991), 181–96.

21. Richard Bednar, Gawain Wells, and Scott Peterson, *Self-Esteem: Paradoxes and Innovations in Clinical Theory and Practice* (Washington, D.C.: American Psychological Association, 1989).

22. Carol Tavris (*Anger: The Misunderstood Emotion*, rev. ed. [New York: Simon & Schuster, 1989], 152–54) holds that the expression of anger is effective under five conditions: (1) it must be directed at the right target; (2) it must restore one's sense of justice and sense of control over the situation (here she says that the expression of anger must "inflict appropriate harm on the other person," something with which I profoundly disagree); (3) the result must be a change in the behavior of the target or increased insight on the part of the person expressing anger; (4) both parties must speak the same anger language; and (5) there must be no angry retaliation from the target.

Women who learn from Tavris's work risk having their anger muted if they agree with her when she asks: "Why is everyone so quick to admire the male ideal? What's so good about it? Why aren't we trying to get men to follow the female pattern, and become less aggressive, hostile, and challenging?" (211). Less hostile, yes, but less aggressive and challenging? I believe that would result in less change and less justice.

23. Saul D. Alinsky, *Rules for Radicals: A Practical Primer for Realistic Radicals* (New York: Vintage Books, 1972) and *Reveille for Radicals* (New York: Random House, 1989).

24. Dorothy Wilt, "Treatment of Anger," in Thomas, *Women and Anger*, 235.

25. C. Welton Gaddy, *When Life Tumbles In: A Handbook for Coping* (Louisville: Westminster John Knox Press, 1993), 74.

Epilogue

1. Beverly Wildung Harrison, "The Power of Anger in the Work of Love: Christian Ethics for Women and Other Strangers" in *Making the Connections: Essays in Feminist Social Ethics*, ed. Carol S. Robb (Boston: Beacon Press, 1985), 3–21.

INDEX OF AUTHORS